Snorkelhead

Adventures in Creek Snorkeling

Keith Williams

Copyright © 2016 Keith Williams

All rights reserved.

ISBN: 0-9975312-0-7
ISBN-13: 978-0-9975312-0-6

Publisher's Note: The experiences portrayed in this book are based on actual events, however the details of those events have been changed to protect the identities of parties involved.

Cover design: Dana Delamar
www.ByYourSideSelfPub.com

Editing: Christine Stewart
The Real Writer Editing Services

Print Formatting: By Your Side Self-Publishing
www.ByYourSideSelfPub.com

No part or the whole of this book may be reproduced, distributed, transmitted or utilized (other than for reading by the intended reader) in ANY form (now known or hereafter invented) without prior written permission by the author, except by a reviewer, who may quote brief passages in a review. The unauthorized reproduction or distribution of this copyrighted work is illegal, and punishable by law.

DEDICATION

This book is dedicated to the pioneer river snorkelers, those people committed to sharing the amazing underwater worlds of our rivers and streams with anyone who will listen. Jeremy Monroe, Jim Herrig, Casper Cox, Russ Ricketts, Dave Herasimtschuk, and Derek Wheaton have especially encouraged me in my snorkeling journey. And it's dedicated to my parents, George and Jane Williams, who never stifled my wonderings about streams.

CONTENTS

Preface 1
1. Human Attachment 3
    Return to Childhood Places 3
    Beginner Snorkel 8
    Stories of My Death Are Greatly Exaggerated 11
    No Child Left Inside 15
    Human Attachment 19
2. Surprise Encounters 21
    Beavers 21
    Toads 22
    Frogs 23
    Turtles 25
    Snakes 27
    Leaves 28
    Algae 29
    Hellbenders 31
    Lamprey 32
    Mussels 34
    Worlds, Rocked 36
3. Impacts 39
    Life Finds a Way 39
    Turbidity 41
    Floods 45
    Nuclear Shadow 47
    Fish Declines 50
    Rock Snot 51
    Dams 52
    Trash 56
4. Migration 58
    Eels 58
    Circle of Life 60
    That's Not a Shad 64
5. Fish 67
    Mouth with a Tail 67
    Sunny Entertainment 68
    Darting Rainbows 69
    Nothing Common about the Common 71
    The Joy of Trout 73
    Rainbow Ballet 76
    Invasive Strength and Agility 77
6. Risks and the Power of Water 79
    Into the Wash 79
    Night 83
    Screaming Barfies 86
    Waterfall Pool 91
    Flying Wild Rivers 93
7. We Have Come Too Far 95
About the Author 98

Preface

My dad gave me my first underwater experience. I stood on a rock in water over my head wearing a mask and snorkel, too afraid to put my head in the water. He gently nudged me off the rock so I had no choice but to look below.

A whole other world was revealed. An incredible jungle of underwater vegetation with leaves of all sizes and shapes and textures filled the bottom of this small lake. The few gaps that existed in the vegetation were filled with schooling sunfish. That little nudge off the rock sent me flying over an aquatic jungle canopy and I've never been the same since. I spent the first part of my adult life exploring marine environments. I dove the Great Barrier Reef, the coral triangle in Palau, and Caribbean mangroves. I forgot about the amazing freshwater world.

Seven years ago, I saw RiverWebs, a movie that tells the story of a pioneering Japanese scientist, Shigeru Nikano. His science was rooted in making observations while snorkeling streams. This reminded me of the experiences I had snorkeling rivers and streams as a kid and I decided to explore our rivers and streams as an adult. I knew creeks since I'd grown up exploring them, studied them in college and grad school, but had never thought to intentionally explore beneath their surface. Shigeru Nakano's story inspired me to snorkel my local rivers and streams.

I stood on the bank of the Big Elk Creek in north eastern Maryland and debated for 30 minutes before finally rationalizing that, since I was here, I might as well get in the water. But I was still reluctant as I pulled my gear bag from my car that I'd parked on a busy street in the largest town in my region. I didn't want people to see what I was doing. I felt a little embarrassed that I was about to lay down in water just deep enough to float on, to look for life in a river most consider to be a polluted waste with no value.

Creek snorkeling seems odd because it involves snorkeling in water barely knee deep in creeks most people think don't contain life worth watching. When people think of snorkeling, they think of tropical reefs, not temperate creeks. So what would I say if someone asked what I was doing? It felt similar to wearing a life jacket in the bath tub. But the section of the Elk Creek I'd chosen had a good veil of trees shielding it from the full view of nonstop traffic on Cecil Avenue. The parts of the Big Elk I knew, just less than a mile downstream from that spot, were pretty well degraded due to an urbanized watershed. I figured that the effort of donning my wet suit would be largely wasted. But I was there with my gear and said out loud, "What else are you going to do with this sunny day if you don't stick your head in this water?" and suited up.

I found a completely unexpected, hidden world in this stream. Bright green aquatic moss covered rocks. Hydropsyche caddis fly webs were spun between the rocks and in the moss, and large schools of big shiners fed in the current. When people think about this, or any, neighborhood creek, most picture what I'd assumed was beneath the surface here: a pretty desolate stream without much life, and certainly nothing attractive.

But when I took a closer look, in spite of my stereotypical view of this suburban creek, a whole new world, vibrant with life, was revealed. And by taking the time to look even closer, layers of life within life were revealed. It just took a slight change in perspective to challenge the stereotypes I held about this creek, which has led to a change in how I view all suburban and urban streams. Our creeks contain diversity and dazzling beauty, and incredible natural acts are happening in all of them.

It was in this moment that I realized I really didn't know rivers and streams. I'd spent my life in them, studied them, conducted research in them, but didn't really know these common environments on their own terms. I never took the time to see them from their perspective. I learned about fish by hauling them out of the water (their medium) into air (my medium). I learned how to identify them from decades old specimens preserved in yellowed jars. Live fish, in their environment are so different, so much more vibrant, there's much more depth to these animals than just a common or scientific name. There are complex behaviors and interactions; each species seems to have its own kind of personality.

It was in this moment, during this first creek snorkeling trip, that I decided to explore and document the wonders of our freshwater rivers and streams and help other people realize and appreciate that they are astonishing underwater communities that can't be judged from the surface.

A few years later I was reminded of this purpose while snorkeling a stream in the Thomas Jefferson National Forest. I saw a candy darter, an ornately colored fish with bright orange yellow and turquoise bands on its body that looks like it belongs in the Amazon much more than in a small Virginia stream. Most people don't know they even exist, and this is why I snorkel streams and rivers and document what I see. To protect amazing sights like this. To protect the diversity that remains in our freshwaters. There were other fish in this creek as well—mountain red-bellied dace and crayfish. Seeing them gave me the same thrill I felt when I saw the candy darter. The same thrill I'd felt when I snorkeled with the smallmouth earlier that morning, the shad that spring, and the sunnies every summer. There are things of worth and beauty in our streams, and we need to work to protect them all. I want my kids and grandkids to have the same opportunities I did to see these incredible stream-scapes and witness the drama, struggles, and splendor of freshwater life. I want the seventh generation to have more of these opportunities than we do today. This book is the first report on my mission.

But this book is more than an underwater accounting of what lives in our rivers and streams. It explains how our freshwaters have shaped me, and how integral they are to my life. I am a father to three kids. Creek snorkeling has become infused in all aspects of my life. My family and I enjoy snorkeling as recreation, the way some families go fishing or go to the beach. It's also work. I am an outdoor educator and snorkeling has become a pillar experience in our program. Taking people snorkeling in a river for the first time is a special privilege for me. Finally, creek snorkeling is also refuge. I also work as a paramedic, and rivers help me sort out the daily tragic EMS experiences. This book tries to relay all of this, and I hope it inspires you to explore your local stream.

1. Human Attachment

Return to Childhood Places

I grew up on creeks. We lived on Hawthorne Avenue in Colonia, NJ, which backed onto the Pumpkin Patch Creek. The Pumpkin Patch is a tributary to the Rahway River, which is the major river entering the Arthur Kill, which in turn forms part of the Hudson Raritan estuary complex. I visited the creek daily, in all weather. The Pumpkin Patch was where I was a master crayfish fisher and knew their life cycle by being a part of it. The Pumpkin Patch, at least my section of it, started from three storm sewer outfall pipes at Public School #22, flowed through the last remaining patch of woods in a suburbanized part of New Jersey, trickled over a concrete lined channelized section where algal mats grew thick, to my deep hole that was even too deep for me to venture into. Calf boots, hip boots, chest waders, all were successfully flooded by me in all seasons so my mother gave up trying to keep me dry.

I knew each rock and every riffle. I knew which rock held what crayfish. I knew where the big ones were. I knew the flood-scoured, carved clay bottom that formed the deep gorge where the big suckers lived, at the end of the concrete channelized part. I'd watch the rainbow gas and oil spill slicks bend and flow on the surface around rocks and down gentle riffles. The smell of diesel mixed with clay- heavy mud as bull dozers and excavators straightened the stream and laid rock into gabion baskets to keep the creek in its channel, and to keep the channel from moving. I knew what the creek had looked like before the houses were there, when the forest was intact, when the stream was allowed to act like a stream and flood its banks from time to time and change the course of its channel.

Mrs. Beck lived across the creek in a Tudor style house that she and her husband Karl had built from materials they harvested from the local forest and creek. Ruth and Karl Beck had escaped Nazi Germany and were the first to build in the woods off of Inman Avenue, before my street, Hawthorne Avenue, was even a muddy smudge. The fireplace and chimney were made from round, water smoothed red, gray, brown and rust colored rocks they'd collected from the creek. All the lumber, the plank paneling, exposed beams, and hard wood flooring had been milled from oaks they'd cut in the course of clearing their homesteading site. Mrs. Beck's description of the area when they first arrived captivated me—no other houses and Inman Avenue had been a pothole filled dirt road. But what really grabbed my interest were her stories about the creek. Mrs. Beck's blue eyes sparkled behind her small gold-framed glasses as she described how the creek had run clearer and deeper then. She told stories of how she and Karl had fished as many huge trout out of the cold water as they could possibly use and took pictures of Karl holding stringers full of large trout down from the mantle to show me examples of the bounty that once was. I could barely imagine the area covered in forest, with her house and one-half acre garden patch the only clearing instead of all houses and streets and lawns of my day. I couldn't imagine that kind of bounty coming from the

1970's Pumpkin Patch. The best I could do was catch four inch crayfish and foot long suckers. That's all that was there, and I considered this to be abundance, but I still dreamed of a day when the Pumpkin Patch would be restored. When the water ran clear and cool and native trout again topped the food chain.

My love of streams comes from this degraded little creek, from Mrs. Beck who passed her strong love of and connection with nature on to me, and especially my parents, who never questioned my enthusiasm for streams. Snorkeling a creek on their February anniversary is a good way for me to celebrate and remember them.

My dad introduced me to rivers. We camped on their shores, fished their waters, canoed their rapids and snorkeled in them. He took SCUBA classes with me in 7th grade. I remember feeling nervous as we sat in the water waiting for the instructor to come and get us when it was our turn to perform the required skills underwater. While many people anticipated reaching the barren rocky bottom in about 50 feet of water during the checkout dive, I enjoyed swimming through the shallower depths where there was more life, and my dad and I chose to spend more time diving the alive shallows than the barren depths. My parents always supported me being in a creek. They fostered my love for streams and I miss them terribly, so a fitting tribute is to get into the water, to explore.

Stoney Creek is a non-descript suburbanizing stream. And it has the typical features you would expect to see where houses are taking over woods. The stream is far from pristine, and while it's not filled with trash, it isn't clean. Stream corridors make convenient routes for sanitary sewer mains, and Stoney Creek isn't any different. Manhole monuments of concrete and steel rise five feet above the floodplain. Amtrak trains scream though a thin veil of woods that hides them from sight, and the back of a new shopping center perches on a hill overlooking the stream. A homeless encampment of three tents sits in the skinny strip of woods between the creek and shopping center. It's a typical stream, tucked into the folds of suburbia and forgotten.

I slipped beneath the surface, and as usual a whole new world appeared. Algae covered everything and created an otherworldly scene where flowing golden fur glowed in the sunlight everywhere I looked. It was like swimming through a painting of a make believe world. While the view was interesting, it was also expected. That much algal growth is a sign of an over-fertilized creek, and most of our suburban streams are over-fertilized by nutrients that run off from our yards and streets.

I figured this trip would be mostly about witnessing incredible streamscapes and geologic architecture rather than seeing life. The water was extremely cold, and after just a few minutes it penetrated my dry suit and insulating layer and chilled through to my skin. Knives of cold stabbed my exposed face the minute I got in the water, and soon my thighs started to sting. I saw a lone caddis fly on a rock, and as I watched the cadis graze, a sculpin darted from under a cobble out into the open.

Sculpin are predatory, and this one had large downturned puffy lips that defined the edges of a mouth that took up most of the fish's face, and a tapered body shape camouflaged in mottled tan and gray. A bright orange band framed the edge of its dorsal fin. It was perfectly constructed to be an ambush predator. This fish lies well-hidden and waits for an unsuspecting darter, or other small fish to wander by, then it explosively snatches the prey.

Sculpin are pretty common in cleaner water, but I had never seen a sculpin in this area, and certainly hadn't expected to see one in this suburbanized, sewer-lined, forgotten stream. This fish, in this creek was special. It was a fish that gave me hope. If a sculpin could be here in this degraded water, there is hope. My parents taught me there is always hope.

Stoney Creek might be suburbanized, it may be forgotten, but this fish is a good reason to remember all the experiences I have had in suburbanizing streams. It's a good reason to continue to explore and witness all the incredibly unexpected sights and natural drama, and to remember the people who have fostered my love for streams, even ones that some would consider unlovable.

The water I explored with my dad was rarely pristine, but always gave me a sense of wonder. One of our favorite places to visit was the New Jersey Pine Barrens, not a snorkeling mecca due to the dark tea-stained water in the rivers that wind through the wilderness. I got a chance to revisit the

Barrens and as soon as I arrived the smell of pine opened a flood of memories. It had been a while since I had been there. I'd spent summers there growing up. The Jersey Pine Barrens have always held a special place in my heart. Maybe because my parents first took us camping there. Maybe because it was where I first tasted adult freedom. First in the form of solo early morning bike rides on deserted roads as whippoorwills called while the rest of my family slept, then as unsupervised canoe trips down the tannin waters of the Mullica and Batsto rivers. I miss those days, and the people I shared them with.

I could feel my heart beat just a little faster as I geared up from the usual expectancy of exploration. Snorkeling the Mullica is not like a first attempt on Everest, or a challenger deep descent to the oceanic abyss. But this was new territory for me. Creek snorkeling often gives me that small jolt of exploratory excitement. While rivers and streams are familiar to us, their underwater views are not. I used to feel at home in the barrens but that time I was a stranger. After three decades the barrens weren't as familiar and landmarks didn't register.

The barrens had always been a mystical place, full of lore and legend, and I often looked over my shoulder. It's the home of the Jersey Devil, a kind of centaur beast, part Satan, part human. There are a ton of stories about the Jersey Devil; supposedly it was born after Satan and a witch had a little tryst. It's supposed to roam the barrens and steal the souls of those it encounters. Every year there are reports of sightings. I've had a few run-ins with the devil, real or imagined. Once, while driving through the barrens on my way to the ocean in the dark hours before dawn, I needed to use the bathroom. I pulled my car onto the shoulder of an empty road and took a few steps into the pine and oak barrens forest to relieve myself. I heard rustling through the leaves and chalked it up to a squirrel. They always sound bigger at night. But then I realized it wasn't a continuous rustling like squirrels make. I was listening to bipedal steps through the leaves and they were getting closer. I suddenly lost the urge, and jumped back into my car just as the steps sounded like they were only yards away. A few years later I was canoeing the Batsto River. I got off the water for the night as the sun fell from the sky and cast shadows over the river. I lit a small fire and started to cook dinner. I looked up from the pot I was stirring and saw two red eyes 50 yards away in the woods, staring back. They took off as soon as I saw them and I spent a sleepless night on a sand bar in the river. Now, these experiences made me feel a little uneasy, and I wondered if the Jersey Devil was watching, even though it was two in the afternoon.

In the water, tannins had leached from decaying vegetation and stained the waters to a dark burgundy tea color. I'd never snorkeled dark waters, and didn't know what to expect. Water flowing out of bogs is especially dark. One of the unique aspects of the Pine Barrens is the contrast between adjacent systems: very arid nutrient poor sands interspersed with areas where the aquifer surfaces and forms bogs. There was a bog located just upstream so I couldn't see the bottom of the few foot deep Mullica as I reluctantly stuck my head under the water.

The water was clear but dark and being there was a little unnerving. Everything was tinted red, as if there was a crimson lens in my mask. It was like swimming through the set of a horror film, with everything under a red light. The stream-scape was interesting, at least what I could see of it. Sand bars looked orange striped and some kind of underwater grass grew from the cut bank of the river like fine green hair. I didn't see any fish at first, and the dark water made me want to cut my search short. My vivid imagination, fueled by images from popular television shows about freshwater river monsters, coupled with the feeling of being watched by the Jersey Devil, almost made me abort.

But I persisted, looking under overhanging root masses. Some kind of fish came shooting out from behind a veil of roots and flew over my shoulder. I laughed at my fright after the water settled, and watched a few male sunnies try to shoo me away from their nests. I didn't see much, but still I was glad I'd gotten in. I could say I'd tried to snorkel in tannin stained water that had given me a different perspective of a very different kind of stream.

While I spent a few weekends a year in the barrens, I spent my high school years on and in the Delaware. Going back to this river was very different than visiting the barrens. This felt familiar, almost like no time had passed.

I know the Delaware river-scape. It's the river of my youth. I fished, tubed, and dived in its waters. I hiked and camped its shores, canoed and kayaked its surface. But life happens, and I moved to the Susquehanna River where I've been exploring for the last 20 years.

It had been 16 years since I'd been back, when I had to clean out and close on my father's house. It was surreal. Everything had been left exactly the way it was the day he died in the upstairs bedroom. I avoided the place, and procrastinated cleaning out the house until I had to. The house was empty and quiet, but full of all the stuff a family acquires over 30 years. My sister had come in before me and taken special mementoes, but the rest of the stuff remained. Sorting through everything brought back memories and intensified my grief. I didn't want to be there cleaning it out.

My parents died six months apart, and even though a lot of time has passed, the empty pain is still there. I don't remember the closing of its sale, outside of feeling like I really didn't want to sell the house. But I remember going to the river afterward to sort things out, to help me make sense of this next parentless stage in my life. I haven't been back since and 16 years later most of the people from my childhood were gone and I found myself missing them all as I prepared to get into the Delaware. In some ways this felt like a homecoming. In some ways I felt like an uninvited guest.

The bottom in that small reach of the Delaware drops into deep eddy wormholes. It was late winter, and I wasn't used to big water this time of year. Most of the large rivers ran murky right about now, but the Delaware remained relatively clear. I took advantage of a rain free week to get in and explore for as long as the cold water would allow.

I was hoping for some fish, maybe an eel or two, possibly a remnant shad, but what I got was incredible architecture. A fractured bedrock outcrop pinched the water into flumes between blocks, and the force of the entire Delaware River funneled into a dozen gaps in the rock. Finer gravels and Asian clam shells accumulated in the eddies behind angulated slabs. The bedrock was covered in algae and sponges that made it look painted.

I couldn't get over the vastness of the river. I was slowly heading out toward the middle but still only explored a tiny part near the Pennsylvania shore. There was one hundred feet of river between me and the New Jersey side, and I could only see 20 feet of it at a time. Swimming big water is always a little unnerving for me. It feels risky. It exposes me to the forces of the river and reminds me that I really am helpless against them. I can work with them, but if I go against them I will lose. Snorkeling big water is humbling and grounding. Water can be dangerous, but the real threats are those we pose to the Delaware, and all rivers. Things like excess nutrients, sediments, toxic wastes and runoff. Dams. When I started back toward the Pennsylvania side I saw a cluster of sticks walk over the bedrock below and realized it was a caddis fly. These insects cement twigs and pebbles together to make a protective case. A few snails also grazed. I didn't see any fish. None of the expected players. But the geology—the biology that encrusts the geology—and most basic forces made this short exploration a memorable shaping experience.

Not far upstream is Cooks Creek, which empties into the Delaware at the site of an old industrial complex. The buildings are long gone but the railroad tie and concrete slab reinforced 30 foot tall creek walls, abundant slag in the creek bed, and canal and road bridges high above stand as reminders to the site's industrial past. When I lived there, there were rumors of hazardous waste contamination of this place when the buildings stood, and that thought made me a little nervous to stick my face in the water.

I slipped into the Delaware just upstream of the Cooks Creek confluence. Thick, unnatural algae covered everything, in unnaturally warm water. I drifted downstream and saw thermal waves where the cold Cooks Creek water met the warm stagnant eddy water. The heavy brown fur that covered everything, the rapid plunge to a bottom scattered with industrial chunks of concrete, and the thermal waves gave the place an eerie feel.

A boat motored by and the algae that blanketed the bottom shook free in the wake and formed a cloud of flocculent crap. I was swimming in crud. The last time I'd been in that part of the Delaware it had been clear, and I'd eagerly anticipated the same conditions but had been disappointed.

I saw a huge river chub in Cooks Creek under the canal bridge with a large sore on its head. Another chub had an ulcer rotted through its operculum gill cover. Creepy and concerning, but I couldn't really point to the cause. I couldn't believe this stretch of the Delaware was so degraded. I made a few drifts into and out of the cold Cooks Creek water and started to notice fish. Large smallmouth bass swam in the deeper water. Smaller ones stayed a little shallower and watched me as I watched them. Schools of minnows hung right at the cold/hot interface and fed. One of those schools was satin-finned shiners. I'd only ever seen these as solitary fish, never as a school. Pale blue fins made them look tropical, and watching the school feed made me forget about my creepy surroundings.

One of the best memories I have of the Delaware was a camping/fishing/snorkeling trip my dad and I took to the Delaware Water Gap when I was in middle school. I was first mesmerized by the Delaware's clear water, deep pools, and abundant fish on that trip. Our campsite had been right on the river where a tree had fallen into the water. The river had scoured out a six foot deep hole around the trunk, and sunnies gathered there. My dad and I put on masks and gently eased into the pool to disturb it as little as possible. Pumpkin seeds are an ornately colored kind of sunfish and we watched them go about their aquatic lives, plucking insects from the bottom, and defending territory.

It's been over 26 years since I've been to the Delaware Water Gap with my dad, and I wished he could see what I do on and in rivers now. I was at the Water Gap to run a snorkeling trip with some students as part of a much larger effort by the Delaware Riverkeeper to get kids connected to the Delaware. I'd arrived hours early to remember. I have so many memories tied to this river, this place. It was almost the way I'd pictured it from so long ago. Pit toilets had been replaced with composters. The river looked unchanged. Its surface was calm but obviously moving. The shores were still forested and the silt islands still split the river in two. I slid into the water with the same slight trepidation I have when I enter any large river. This was big water and the feelings of smallness, insignificance, and lack of control were uncomfortable.

The force of the water matted vegetation beds to the cobbles. The bottom faded into the haze of deeper water that gave the river an infinite feel. Large web spinner caddis fly nets folded and billowed in the current. A water snake appeared in mid water before me, bobbed to the surface and dived when it realized I was there. It wedged between the bottom and a rock and almost blended in, and I ended up losing it to the background when it moved to a better hiding spot. They are such misunderstood and victimized animals, often confused with poisonous snakes, and usually stoned to death.

I could have swum with that snake all day if it would have let me. I could have drifted over cobble and submerged vegetation beds all the way to Philadelphia as I reflected on the memories of my father and me on and in water. My dad didn't know it at the time but he was giving me a deep love of rivers. The river still holds the same fascination for me. It was good to get back to the gap. It wouldn't be nearly as long before I was there again. The Delaware partly shaped who I am, and being there was a reminder of that molding. Rivers insert themselves into our lives when we let them. They are so much more than a collection of rock, mud, and fish, so much more than conduits for water. They shape our communities and our lives. They are spiritual places, sacred. As I snorkel them the feelings of connection and flow of time and spirit grow. It's grounding to be face down in a river.

Beginner Snorkel

I love to introduce people to the sport of freshwater snorkeling. It can be as exciting or calming as you make it. Snorkeling reveals worlds hidden below the surface, and is full of adventure and wonder. Freshwater snorkeling relaxes, connects, and centers. It reminds us that we are a part of a much larger whole, and it always puts things in their right perspective for me. It's easy for me to lose total track of time and place when I'm in a river or stream watching and participating in life. I love to share this with as many people as I can.

Every other year or so I run a mid-winter trip for the NorthBay education team to the freshwater springs in Florida. NorthBay is an outdoor education program that serves urban and underserved kids in a five day residential outdoor experience. These educators positively affect 10,000 students a year and the Florida trip is part thank you for the team's hard work, part training in freshwater ecology, but mostly it's a temporary break from the mid-Atlantic cold and time to hang out and recharge. It's also an opportunity to snorkel in some of the most intriguing and clearest waters in North America.

One year there were a few educators on the trip who had never been snorkeling before, or who had only been snorkeling a few times. Sometimes all it takes to get someone in the water is to provide equipment. Sometimes it takes instruction and reassurance. Anyone, with a little coaching and a little time to get used to the gear can enjoy underwater wonders wherever they are. I handed out masks and snorkels and demonstrated how to put them on.

"Just breathe normally through your mouth and put your face in the water."

A few hard breaths and people were in the new world, watching life.

"Remember where your snorkel ends," I cautioned as people got a little adventurous and started to explore on their own. I floated on the surface to make sure everyone was safe and comfortable. I showed one person from our team how to bend at the waist while picking their legs out of the water to effect a surface dive. I loved watching people head to the bottom, and enjoy the freedom that comes from weightless flight as they skimmed over underwater grass beds. It reminded me of the first time I experienced the freedom of underwater flight, and of some of the tribulations I experienced as a beginner snorkeler: a fogged mask, forgetting that my snorkel ended just above my head so that I inhaled some water on an early surface dive, learning how to work with the current instead of against it, feeling awkward and off balance at first but then experiencing a transformative grace and peace that comes over me every time I get into a river now. But mostly watching beginner snorkelers discover the sport the first time affirmed the thrill I feel each time I stick my head underwater in a river. There is always something new to see.

It didn't take long for all of the new snorkelers in our group to explore the springs on their own and come back with comments like "I never swam with fish before." "I can see why you love it" and "I'm hooked." Me too. And one of the reasons I'm hooked is because these reactions aren't dependent on clear warm water. I hear similar responses wherever I take people snorkeling in less clear places like Lower Susquehanna River tributaries when the shad run in April and the river is cold and murky, or Mill Creek, a tiny stream near my house. These creeks produce the same excitement. A few months after the Florida trip I assembled a group of teachers on the bank of Mill Creek. Mill Creek is just a little thing and really doesn't look like much from the road. The creek is only five feet wide and the shallow, six inch deep runs of riffles are interspersed with one to two foot deep pools. But the water is clear and the gravel is clean. I wasn't sure what we would see, but we didn't have many other options. It had been a wet early summer and our eastern rivers were muddy for the most part. Mill Creek was one of the few exceptions.

"I'm not sure what we are going to see today." I told the group of teachers who were there to learn how to engage their students in stream science through snorkeling. "But then I never really know what I'm going to see when I snorkel any stream. That's one of the beauties of it."

This trip was part of a professional development program to show teachers how to engage students in authentic science in their local environment. But I also hoped that this experience would show teachers the value of taking their kids snorkeling in this creek, which was a short walk from the local middle school.

"You want me to lay in that?!" a teacher said as he pointed to the shallow creek after I explained the simple process of creek snorkeling. It hadn't started well, and the dozen teachers stood looking skeptical, their arms folded across their chests as I lay down in the foot deep riffle. I hoped I saw something. I hoped they would follow my lead, but I felt pretty foolish.

Clear water revealed lots of fish once I submerged beneath the reflective surface. Rosy-sided dace competed for a mate. Common shiner fed in the water column. The colors of these fish always impress me, and for a minute I forgot I was in a temperate stream. It looked more tropical. Something hopped from one spot to another on the bottom. I looked down to see a sculpin curved around a smooth round cobble by the current. It let me get a few pictures, then decided I was too close and in an instant disappeared into the background.

I called out what I was seeing through my snorkel, and hoped some of the teachers would join me. Someone came in alongside, then another teacher joined us. It wasn't long before the entire group was in the stream crawling upriver, exploring. A thin tail stuck up from the pebbly bottom and as I suspected, an elver, or baby eel, appeared from the other end of a larger rock. Another sculpin shot off and settled against a round stone. Darters darted and a large sunny challenged us from under woody cover in a deeper hole. Teachers exclaimed their finds through their snorkels and it was satisfying to hear the unintelligible, muffled, excited chatter.

The teacher who had challenged me at the start of the trip approached me as we were packing up.

"Thanks."

"You are welcome. Thanks for getting in."

"I would have never thought to snorkel here."

That's the whole point. It's amazing what lives in even our most forgotten streams. All we need to do is find it by snorkeling. Everyone here was familiar with this creek, but no one *knew* it. They were familiar with the creek, knew it existed, but they had never explored it. They'd never gotten down on its level and immersed themselves in the creek's environment. This trip changed their perspective and gave them a completely new view of a very familiar stream, a view they can now share with their students.

The next summer I was running another professional development workshop with a group of Baltimore City teachers on the shore of the Lower Susquehanna. The group was very eager to get into the water, likely because of the July heat, but either way, I didn't have to work hard to get them into the river. The Susquehanna is big there. Huge and powerful when it wants to be. On this trip the current barely moved. We put on masks and floated over ten foot deep holes of clear water. Most of these teachers had never snorkeled before, but they bravely followed me away from the shore to explore. I saw the whisker of a catfish sticking out from under a large rock shelf on the bottom ten feet below and I called the teachers together.

"I think there is a cat fish down here under this ledge. Let's go to the bottom to see if we can see what kind it is. Maybe it's one of the invasive flatheads we talked about earlier."

Flathead catfish were first identified in the Susquehanna in the early 2000's. They are top predators, grow to a large size, and are expected to have a negative effect on native fish populations. It would be a nice opportunity to observe a fish we talked about in lecture.

We counted to three, held our breath, and dived to the bottom. A few of us grabbed on to the top of the ledge and peered upside down into the dark space between rock and sandy bottom. There wasn't anything obvious, but it was hard to see into the void. I thought I'd made a mistake and hadn't seen a whisker after all. Just as I was about the stick my hand into the shadow, a two foot channel cat exploded out from under the rock and hit me in the mask. We rocketed to the surface, and the catfish followed. It was like the damn thing chased us. I'd never seen behavior in a catfish like that before.

Once the catfish got to within a foot or so of our feet it dropped back to the bottom and we observed it from above. It had fresh punctures in its back and bits of pink flesh hung out over its olive skin. We conjectured that it was snatched by an eagle then dropped. Maybe this explained the odd, aggressive behavior.

We floated and snorkeled and escaped the heat while we explored. We swam under bedrock overhangs and through exposed root wads along undercut banks. We watched minnows school and bass hunt. We saw the current wave through patches of wild celery and water willow. We were all adventurers making new discoveries beneath the surface of the Susquehanna, just minutes after being beginner snorkelers. Rat in Kenneth Grahame's *Wind in the Willows* said "Believe me, my young friend, there is nothing—absolutely nothing—half so much worth doing as simply messing about in boats." If Rat had tried snorkeling, he would amend his list to include absolutely nothing half so much worth doing as simply messing about snorkeling rivers. River snorkeling turns everyone into an explorer, even the beginners.

Stories of My Death Are Greatly Exaggerated

I guess I looked like a body floating in the White Clay Creek. Except I wasn't just floating, I was moving. Upstream, against the current. But still I appreciated that people stopped to make sure that I wasn't dead. I was thankful for all five of the "Are you okay?" I got, and no one called 911 before checking to see that I was in fact not dead. I appreciated that. I appreciated that people stopped to see if anything was wrong. It restored my faith in humanity.

But someone snorkeling in the White Clay Creek should not be the exception, even on the cusp of winter. It should be the norm, so that when people see someone floating in a stream they assume they are watching fish, or appreciating the architecture of the creek, or maybe enjoying the rush of weightless flight through riffles and rapids rather than assuming they're dead. Creek snorkeling shouldn't be that abnormal. There should be hundreds of people creek snorkeling. Hundreds of people should be sticking their faces in the nearest stream to see what's going on, to experience the perceived mundane in extraordinary ways.

I was trying to watch a school of large chubs, and tried harder to get a decent shot of the shy fish. But it was difficult to get lost in the wilderness of the White Clay after the sixth "Hey can you hear me? Are you okay? WHAT are you doing?" followed by my explanation that there really are amazing things to see here, even now. That, really, I'm not crazy, and I'm not dead. On the contrary, I'm very sane and very much alive. Creek snorkeling does that for me. It had been a long six week haul without a day off and those trips kept me sane. Creek snorkeling helps me stay in the here and now, and helps me feel alive. It puts things into perspective.

Maybe I could get these folks into the creek when things warmed up in the spring so they too could experience the weightless solitude, perspective, and discovery that keeps me coming back.

I have even been confused with a dead body in some of the most remote snorkeling locations. I was in a small creek in the Pisgah National Forest, having hiked a mile to get to a deep pool beneath a gorgeous waterfall. I'd slowly explored around large trees that had fallen into the pool. They were great habitat for trout and I was slowly creeping up on a huge butter belly brown that sat on a red bedrock shelf just upstream of the large trunk. I thought I heard quick steps through dry leaves but dismissed it. The chances of someone else being here were slim. I heard the rustling again and thought maybe it was a black bear. I lifted my head out of the water just before a concerned hiker jumped into the stream. He screamed. I screamed.

"Man! I thought you were dead!"

"Sorry about that. I'm just watching some trout. Thanks for the concern though."

He looked a little embarrassed as he hiked off, and I was a little reluctant to get back in. I didn't want to startle someone else.

I once almost caused a car accident. I was in the Octoraro Creek near a bridge in the middle of winter. I heard brakes screech and yelling. Someone had stopped in the middle of the bridge to see if I really was a dead body, and a second vehicle almost rear ended the first, which resulted in an exchange of screamed expletives between the two drivers. I snuck out of the water. Now I check to see if I'm within sight of a road before getting into a river.

But there have been instances when the person floating was in fact dead, and I have been involved with many rescues and recoveries in my role as a swift water rescue technician and paramedic. The river I snorkel has regularly been the site of numerous drownings.

One night we were dispatched for the water rescue on the Susquehanna River in the area of Sterett Island. I found one of the boat's occupants clinging to a rock. He looked pale and was quiet.

"We were anchored right over there." He pointed up river. "We anchored from the back and water came over the stern and the boat sank. My friend couldn't swim. He didn't have a life vest on." He started to cry.

I didn't know what to say. I never do. Instead I directed our team to search further upriver. We found the 20 year-old the next day.

I was called in one night when another 20 year-old tried to swim for shore after his canoe capsized at night.

"Two souls in the water. Caller states he is in the middle of the river between Lapidum and Lees Landing. People on shore can hear yelling. No life vests," The dispatcher announced.

This was the real deal. This is what we train for. My foot stepped harder on the gas. I got to the boat ramp at the same time as our first rescue boat and headed into the river. We found one occupant hanging on to the floating lid of a cooler and pulled him into the boat.

"He said he was going to swim for it," he told us. "He let go of the cooler and started to swim toward Lees Landing. I heard him scream for help right before you got me."

The rest of the river was quiet. We searched the area we suspected was the last point known. The state police helicopter lit up the river with its massive flood light. Six other boats flashed yellow and red emergency lights as they idled up and down and across the river. Boats, ground crews, and the helicopter searched the shoreline in the remote chance he had swum to shore. We sent a sheriff's deputy to his address with the hope that he'd not only made it to shore but walked home. There was no answer at the door.

After an hour and a half, the operation changed from a rescue to a recovery; there was no hope of this young man being alive. We regrouped in a nearby marina to discuss ending the search. All teams agreed it was time to call it off for the night. I knew the family was in the area, but didn't know who they were.

"Why aren't you searching?' a woman asked as we walked past. No one answered.

"Why aren't you searching?' she asked again as I walked by. I didn't want to respond. I didn't want to engage in her grief.

"Why aren't they talking to me?" she sobbed to someone with her.

"Ma'am, can I answer your question?" I asked. She at least deserved some answers. I wasn't sure I had the bravery to face her, but I tried.

"Why are all the boats here? Why aren't you searching?!?" she cried.

"Ma'am we are developing a new plan. We have been searching for an hour and a half and haven't found anything."

"Where is the helicopter?" she said.

"It was here. It searched for an hour and had to return."

"It's coming back right?!"

"No ma'am, the helicopter has done all it could."

"How many people are searching?"

"We have eight boats out, probably about 50 people."

"Are you looking on the shore? Why aren't you looking on the shore? My son! You don't know my son! He could be on one of those islands. He could hike through that thick brush. You need to send someone over to Harford County!"

"We have teams over there ma'am."

"How cold is the water?"

"Seventy two degrees."

"See! That's not bad," said another family member clearly thinking only about hypothermia. They didn't realize that a patient submerged for an hour and a half in 72 degree water has no chance of surviving due to a lack of oxygen to the brain rather than hypothermia. I turned and walked back down the dock.

"Is anyone talking to her? Has anyone started the process of letting her know that he is dead?" I asked our command.

"That's DNR's job."

I wasn't going to argue. I really couldn't handle her grief any more. My heart broke for her. I was frustrated that we had missed him by minutes. If only we'd been a little faster. If only we'd had better information. I could have swum for him from shore.

"Okay Mike. We are going back out for her benefit then," I said as I reached my team's boat. We searched for another two hours to give the family time to come to the realization that their brother and son was in the river and dead. We found him two days later.

But the worst, so far, was a five year old. I was already in my Chief's emergency response truck when the call came in for a drowning one town down river. The dispatcher reported that a five year old had fallen off a dock. I was the closest paramedic and Water Rescue Technician, so I responded, even though I was ten minutes away. I normally drive very cautiously, even when driving with my emergency lights on. But this call was different. A five year old was in the water and we knew almost exactly where. We had a real chance for saving this little boy. I made the ten minute trip in five, grabbed my snorkeling gear and Advanced Life Support equipment and hustled down the dock. One of our deputy chiefs had arrived minutes before. He was in his own boat fishing nearby when he'd heard the call. He and his son were probing the bottom with net handles.

"We think he went in over there." Mike pointed to a spot between floating finger piers that stick out at 90 degree angles to the main dock. "He rode his scooter down the ramp and off the side. The current is strong and I think it's pulling toward me." Mike was on the downstream side of the dock from where the child had gone in. I put on my mask and jumped into the water on the upstream side of the dock, where the boy had fallen off the pier.

There are always hazards on the bottom of the river. Trees, branches, fishing line that can tangle a diver. I took a deep breath, tried to calm my nerves and headed for the bottom ten feet below. The river was quiet here. I could detect my heart beating in my ears. It was completely black, and the strong bottom current whipped my feet over my head, like a scorpion. I kept my chest on the soft bottom and fanned my arms out in wide sweeps as I swam along, completely disoriented. I had no idea which direction I was swimming. I wanted to search in an organized pattern, but in reality it was going to be a series of haphazard surface dives as I hoped to avoid getting snagged on the bottom, or surfacing under the floating pier. I ran out of breath and had to surface. I came up, took a few quick gulps of air and went back under. Nothing.

Out of air again, surfaced and went back down. Each time was shorter under water. Each time I became more exhausted. I was just about done, just about to the point where I physically couldn't do any more when I took one more breath and submerged. I again fanned out my arms. My left hand felt something like a submerged dish towel. I pulled it toward me and it felt more like a waterlogged rag doll. I had him. I shot to the surface.

"I've got him!" I gasped as I swam to the finger pier. I handed the limp boy up and climbed out of the water as members of our team started CPR. I got my paramedic equipment ready and initiated advanced life support interventions with a second paramedic. We put him on our heart monitor to see if we could defibrillate his heart; we intubated him, placing a breathing tube into his lungs so we could oxygenate him, and we started an IV and administered cardiac drugs, hoping to chemically start his heart. None of the interventions worked. The boy remained pulseless while his mother wailed at the other end of the dock. He was the same age as my youngest son, but I couldn't let that register now. I couldn't let any of that emotion get in the way of the tasks we needed to do.

I called the hospital on the radio. "Harford this is Cecil Paramedic 691, en route with a priority one pediatric arrest due to drowning. Estimated in water time 20 minutes. ETA ten minutes. CPR in progress, asystole on monitor throughout, bilateral 20 G IVs established Intubated three rounds epi administered."

We arrived at the hospital and wheeled the boy into the major room, a brightly lit sterile, green tiled room where all serious cases go. The doctors and nurses took over care. They tried as hard as we had, but after another 30 minutes of effort, it was apparent that this boy was dead.

"We have been at this for an hour total with no change. Can anyone think of anything else we should try?" the lead doctor asked. The room was silent.

"Does anyone disagree with stopping resuscitation efforts?" Again silence.

"Time of death 21:35."

The nurse doing compressions stopped, and the buzz of activity stilled. People filed out in silence. A few asked if others were okay when they reached the hallway. The child's mother was brought into the room.

"Oh God no! Don't stop! Please!" she screamed and started to pump on her son's chest.

The doctor assured her that everything possible had been done and he was gone. A nurse held her up.

I could finally let the stoic facade fall and I cried. The ambulance drove me back to my truck, which was parked at the river. I stood on its shores and tried to make sense of it all. I still remember the date of the incident and his birth day. Rivers can take away life but they also put life into perspective and I head to rivers after especially tragic EMS calls.

Big Branch was iced over as I stood on its shores in early January. I had been grieving the loss of a teenage patient for the last few days, since he died on New Year's. He'd been the driver in a vehicle that hit a telephone pole. I was the only medic working at the time of the call—11:33 pm, New Year's Eve. Minutes before the New Year. I arrived by myself and found him pulseless in the driver seat. I removed him from the vehicle and started to work. We got a pulse in the hospital but it only lasted fifteen minutes. The 17 year-old was pronounced dead at 1:00 am on January first and I had spent at least part of each day since trying to figure out why. It never makes sense to me when someone young dies.

But I hadn't come to Big Branch to sort out life's mysteries. My motives were much more simplistic. I'd come because it had been a few weeks since I'd snorkeled one of my favorite creeks. We perceive that life ends when winter starts, but that's far from true. Life is abundant, just a little less noticeable in winter, and the same holds true for the wintertime life in our rivers and streams.

I knew getting into the freezing water was going to be painful, and it was, but the stinging subsided and I relaxed. The water was cold but bearable. Life immediately became apparent. A sculpin darted toward the shoreline and disappeared into the surroundings. This fish is so well camouflaged the only way I would see it again was if it moved, and it didn't. A school of some kind of minnow swam out from under the beginnings of an ice sheet. Two large fall fish came in for a closer look at me. I love these fish. They're big year round chubs, always here in every season, just in different spots. They aren't too skittish, and seem as curious about me as I am about them so we usually end up floating together as we watch each other for a while.

I didn't last too long. The cold forced me to get out just as I lost feeling in my hands. But I was in the water long enough to know that life here was abundant and thriving. Maybe not as much as in summer, but I certainly didn't have to search to find it. The perceived end that winter brings is just that, a perceived end, not a real one.

The trip to Big Branch didn't give me any great perspective on the young man's death. It didn't answer any great universal mystery. But for 30 minutes I didn't think about it, and I got out of the water, reassured that life finds a way, that we are part of a much larger whole, and that it would be okay. There is a reassuring permanence in our streams. Maybe death is like winter, a perceived end, not a real one.

No Child Left Inside

In his book *Last Child in the Woods*, Richard Louv details how the last generation of kids have migrated inside their homes. Part of the problem is standardized tests, and how the results of those tests dictate funding levels for schools, and are often attached to teacher and principal salaries. If something is not directly tied to test preparation, it's cut. So schools are letting their kids spend less time outside as part of their education. The federally mandated No Child Left Behind educational standards included no environmental/outdoor education component. Science wasn't even part of No Child Left Behind. Maybe kids weren't left behind (though that's very debatable) but the outdoors, science, history, and the arts certainly were. This resulted in the No Child Left Inside movement. The new standards (Common Core and Next Generation Science) are a step in the right direction since at least science is included, but there is MORE emphasis placed on standardized testing, and if programs can't prove a direct, positive effect on how students perform on those tests, the program is eliminated.

While there was (and is) a ton of hype and saber rattling about No Child Left Inside, funding for environmental education continues to decline. The No Child Left Inside hype is great, but it is only hype. Some of the education programs NorthBay runs are creek snorkeling programs in response to the building constraints on outdoor education. They are inexpensive and are often run in the local stream, which eliminates the need for busses, which is a significant expense. But sometimes, using the local stream presents its own set of logistical challenges.

Coopers Branch is a tiny impacted waterway, a heavily suburbanized stream. Most of its watershed is impervious road, driveway, and roof top. It drains communities in Catonsville and empties into the Patapsco River at Oella, across the river from Ellicott City. It's tiny, barely five feet wide, and maintains a scant trickle of water. As is typical of urban streams, it swells to ten times its size after even just a small rain. I was skeptical that it would be able to keep 40 snorkeling middle schoolers engaged, but this was their creek, the stream that passes through their neighborhood, that drains chem-lawned yards, so I agreed with their dynamic teacher, that the experience would be worth the risk.

I got lots of strange looks as I schlepped bags of snorkeling gear from Oella up the trolley trail to the snorkeling location.

"Oh! Snorkeling, really?" one teacher asked with a confused look on her face.

"Well, yeah," I said, a little embarrassed. I knew how ridiculous it appeared. "It might not look like much, but just beneath the surface lies a whole different world, possibly full of life, and we're going to explore that," I explained, even though I was also a little skeptical.

I gave instructions, handed out gear, lay down on the bank, and submerged my mask in a deeper pool. There wasn't enough room for me to get all the way in. A school of black-nosed dace took off for cover.

"Hey! Black-nosed dace!" I yelled to the students watching. The surprise of finding fish here transferred to my voice. "Check it out!"

A group of students joined me, and together we started to see all sorts of life: crayfish, black-nosed dace, some kind of minnow, frogs, and water snakes. There wasn't a lot of diversity, as was expected, but life was abundant and the students were excited to discover it. We explored our connection to the creek and the creek's connection to us and how it all fits into the larger world around us. We all came away a little more connected to Coopers Branch, and as usual the view below was unexpected and spectacular. Even in that tiny smudge of a creek.

A few weeks later I was running a trip on a much larger stream. The Octoraro is a tributary to the lower Susquehanna and flows through southeastern Pennsylvania and northeastern Maryland. I led a trip with fifth graders from the local elementary school a mile from the creek.

Twenty five students shrieked as they tried to lay down in the cold water. There was a lot of splashing and stomping around, but not much snorkeling. The water got murky fast from the sediments that were re-entrained off the bottom. I started to think the whole thing was a failure. But then I heard comments like "This is the best trip ever!" and "Hey look at the eel!" And while every kid didn't spend all of the time in the river, most did, and most looked around. A lot saw some cool things, like elvers and darters. It was in that moment that I realized the trip was successful in connecting students to their creek.

The most exciting discovery were the elvers—baby eels—migrating back up the Octoraro. They stayed low in the cobble which let them move against the strong current but this usually meant we just got glimpses of the back half of their bodies. Eels reproduce in the Sargasso Sea, an area of the Atlantic Ocean that is defined by a large circular ocean current, bordered by the Gulf Stream on the west, the North Atlantic Current on the north, the Canary Current to the east, and the Atlantic equatorial current to the south. These babies are the young returning to the Octoraro to live in this creek for the next 25 years, when it will be their turn to migrate down river to the Sargasso.

Watching the next generation of both species getting to know the Octoraro made me optimistic, and I hope they both keep returning to the Octortaro. Even with successful trips like this one, it is easy for me to get discouraged with the constant struggle to keep our rivers healthy, and to keep kids in them. But snorkeling with students usually puts things back into their right perspective.

Another trip to Deer Creek reminded me of this. The trip came at the end of a week that wasn't very hopeful. Earlier in the week, an expert panel of marine scientists convened by the International Programme on the State of the Ocean determined that marine life is at significant risk for extinctions never before seen in human history due to over fishing, pollution, and climate change. From the 2013 report: "The central messages from the workshops are that the risks to the ocean and ecosystems it supports have been significantly underestimated; that the extent of marine degradation as a whole is greater than the sum of its parts; and that it is happening at a much faster rate than previously predicted."

The report concluded "that the threats to the ocean were progressing faster with an accelerated rate of change, bigger in scale, and closer in time in terms of the impacts being felt" than previously estimated. I'm not much for alarmist environmentalism, but there is some good science behind this report. The same concerns apply to our freshwater systems.

It had also been a little depressing to snorkel in my region. I hadn't seen clear water for a month. We'd had a flashy weather pattern that spring where localized storm bursts flushed sediments into the streams, because of the poor choices we made on land. Forests and marsh can absorb these downpours without much mud entering our streams. Farm field, lawn, rooftop, and driveway can't, so our streams turn to chocolate milk instantly after a rain, and drive visibilities to mere inches for days. I still snorkel, and am still amazed at what I see when I go, but it's nowhere near as good as it could be.

The clincher was when I witnessed a family stoning a northern water snake to death on Deer Creek. The father hoisted a basketball sized cobble above his head and smashed it on the snake's head just as I walked to the river. His kids tossed baseball sized rocks at the dead snake's body for good measure.

"What did you do that for?' I asked, trying to contain my anger.

"That was a copperhead!" the man said with a cigarette hanging from the corner of his mouth.

"No, it was a water snake, completely harmless."

"No it ain't. I'm from here, and I know a copperhead when I see one!"

Ignorant ass. I really questioned the value of time spent doing environmental education in rivers and streams. That family spent time on a creek and obviously didn't care about the life that's there.

But a Susquehanna River snorkeling trip with a group of Baltimore City high school students combated my pessimism. I met the group of interns from the National Aquarium in Baltimore on the Susquehanna River. These students educated aquarium visitors about our rivers, estuaries and oceans, and I was going to try to increase their first-hand experience of the Susquehanna so that they could maybe impart a little of that awe to aquarium visitors.

"That water is nasty," declared one of the girls.

High school students act tough because they think they are too cool to show enthusiasm. Coupled with being in the river, an environment very foreign to these students, and their perception that the water is dirty, it looked like the day would be a struggle. I didn't know where to start.

"It is a little muddy," I agreed. "But where does this mud come from?"

"The watershed," another student answered, and that launched us into a great conversation about how what we do on land affects water and how what we do in life affects the people around us and the environment. The students started to trust me and let me lead them on a snorkeling exploration between rock outcroppings on the lower Susquehanna. They were versed in the issues killing our streams and the Chesapeake: sediments, nutrients, and invasive species, and they are acting to educate on these topic. Now these student interns can share what it is like to snorkel the Susquehanna with the people they educate. These students are the next wave of environmentalists working to protect the environment, which by default protects our health, and that day they restored my faith in the future. But not every trip goes as well as this one did, and sometimes it's a struggle to get kids engaged.

I had an experience like this on the Big Elk, which rarely disappoints, and that day was no different. I counted eight species of fish within the first ten minutes in the water. The problem was that I was the only one in the water while 20 high school environmental science students watched from the shore.

We had plenty of gear for everyone to get in and see the underwater world of the Elk for themselves. We'd talked about this trip for a month leading up to the day. Even the weather cooperated with a sunny 80 degrees.

My excitement at the diversity and abundance of fish: darters, white suckers, common shiners in breeding color, and the sighting of the more maligned ones like eels coaxed a few students in but still we only had three students finally decide to gear up and get in.

I was disappointed with my inability to convince these students to get in the water to check out what was below the surface, to challenge and expand their view of the Big Elk. To form connections that I hoped would translate into action. I'd never had a student snorkeling trip where so few of them got into the water. Most times I have to work to get them out of the creek, and I wondered why this trip was different. It turned out there was a mix of reasons. Some students had to go to a different class afterward and didn't want to go there wet. Others weren't prepared to get in the water.

But the one reason that was most disturbing was the concern that getting into the Big Elk would make them sick. Maybe we've done too good of a job talking about problems so people perceive that the environment, especially the environment where we live, is damaged to the point of being unhealthy for us. Maybe we have presented a hopeless situation.

If creek snorkeling is about anything, it's about hope. Witnessing a diversity of fish and the struggles of ecology in our local streams, the same streams many people consider to be disease-causing, void, lifeless, and sick, proves that while our actions have impaired our waterways, it's far from too late. It's time for hope to generate action. For hope to maintain the amazing ecosystems that still thrive in our streams, and even restore them to an improved condition.

Above all there is hope. We can work to make our world a better place, and that work can start with the local stream. There's a vibrant ecosystem in the Big Elk Creek, and we can work to protect and restore it. I owed those students that lesson, and it's something I share with students on most trips. But most of the time I'm inspired by the kids I take into rivers and streams; they are the ones giving me hope.

On another trip, a group of fifth graders stood on the shore of the Brandywine beneath signs that say the water contains unhealthy levels of fecal coliform after rains, and fish caught there shouldn't be eaten. Not surprising, since I was at the Brandywine in downtown Wilmington. It's the norm for any urban stream, unfortunately. You wouldn't know it from the surface. It was a picturesque spot, and certainly didn't look impaired.

We asked the fifth graders to form a circle around a picnic table and introduced the day's activities. We were going to determine the health of the Brandywine by looking for benthic macroinvertebrates, organisms that live on the bottom, mostly insects, which tell us so much about water quality. The presence of some kinds of benthic macroinvertebrates indicates great water quality, while the presence of others means horribly unhealthy conditions. We had the kids predict the water quality of the Brandywine with thumb votes. Most pointed down, including mine.

The kids instantly stood in the river, even though the air and water temperatures were in the 50s. Most had boots. Some didn't but that didn't matter and it wasn't long before a student fell in, but came up laughing in the knee deep water. They loved searching for life and were instantly connected to the Brandywine even though most had never been to the river before. I couldn't keep up with excited requests. "Mr. Keith what is this?!" "Mr. Keith check this out!" The hour flew by.

Amazingly these students found organisms that typically need pretty clean water to live. The Brandywine isn't a trout stream. But it's not a cesspool either, and there is a lot to celebrate and be thankful for. Including those Wilmington fifth graders.

The trip came at a time when I was just about to give up on river snorkeling. After a summer of muddy water, coupled with the frustration of some cancelled trips, it just seemed that creek snorkeling was a futile idea. Those kids proved me wrong. I was supposed to inspire the group to take action, but they inspired me to continue on the stream path I'd started years ago.

I can't wait to take more students snorkeling, so we can document the underwater world of the Brandywine, and spread the inspiration that comes from exploring amazing rivers.

Human Attachment

The water in Deer Creek seemed like it had risen and it was a little less clear than the previous week. I figured it had rained upstream somewhere. But based on the hydrograph that shows water flow at different times of the day, the water level had dropped in the last 24 hours.

The water had definitely warmed since my last visit, and I barely noticed the cold when I stuck my face in the rapid. I ferried across the swift current into the lee of the large rock that last week had sheltered adult caddis flies heading back into the water. I expected to see more of this phenomenon, but things change fast in a stream. There were no caddis to be found. Instead the entire back of the rock was covered in bulbous sculpin eggs. At least that's what I thought they were. Sculpin are primarily nocturnal predators, and I would love to watch this egg laying process in the wild. Now I knew when to look—the week before St. Patrick's Day.

I drifted out from the protection of the rock into the main flow. A slab of gray wriggling into a gap between rocks on the bottom caught my eye. I stopped, turned, and crawled upstream against the stiff current. Two of the largest eels I have ever seen were going after something under one of the large cobbles in the rapid. Were they hunting together? Or was each one out for itself? It sure seemed like they were working in tandem.

I continued to crawl upstream against the heavy current into the large pool above the rapid. Even the flow there was strong. Much of the eddy in the pool had been embedded by sand moved from upstream during some of the heavy flows the past winter and late fall. The only thing certain about streams is that they change. I am attached to that pool. Joyce and I raised our family there. It's the local swimming hole. I brought my daughter Gracie to that pool when she was six months old. I taught my sons how to fish and snorkel there. Gracie helped me lead a snorkeling trip there for the first time this summer. And each time I come back it is different with more memories, different structure, different life, life doing things I can't explain and don't expect. I head out into the main flow and let the current carry me. I scare a huge carp as much as it scares me and it shoots upstream. I drift over a small advanced school of a dozen shad and they peel off to the right. Thousands will soon follow.

The current quickens as the stream bed comes up. Water is forced over rocks and I am dragged with it, like a leaf in the current. I can correct my course here and there, but I am largely at the mercy of the river. Good reminder for life. I eventually reach an eddy which spins me into still water. I leave Deer Creek elated and feeling very much alive.

River snorkeling keeps me grounded and I don't feel like myself when I go for long periods of time without getting into a creek to snorkel. One year I didn't go into the water at all for five months. A few factors led to the dry hiatus, and I really started to question the point of it all. Water stayed murky late into the summer, so visibilies never really got good. The more I questioned why, the more it seemed that human existence, even at its most basic simple level equaled impaired waters. What actions could creek snorkeling possibly inspire that would improve water quality if human existence impaired it? Thunderstorms dumped rain, rivers got muddy and flooded, water levels slowly receded, and the mud settled. But the small windows of clear water seemed to always conflict with my schedule, so I finally conceded to "what's the point," and quit trying.

I felt the effects of not being in water. Water is so primal to our existence. We need it physiologically, and I need it spiritually, so after five months without being in a creek I started to feel disjointed, ungrounded, and floundering on land. I decided it was time to jump back in.

I stood on the bank of Basin Run on an early November afternoon. I knew the water was going to be cold, and wasn't sure what to expect. There had been a lot of big flows between the last time I'd been there and that moment, including the largest rainfall event since Hurricane Agnes in 1972. I expected things would be different and not necessarily for the better, but this spot on the side of the creek still felt like home.

The stabbing sensation of frigid water on my face and hands felt comfortable. There weren't the mounds of sediment I'd expected after the heavy runoff we'd had over the summer. There weren't the cobbles smothered by sands and gravels. The bottom, while different, was the same as I remembered it: cobbles and boulders, clean of sediment and sand. I pushed upstream against the swift current and fresh cold water shot down the front of my wet suit. I crested a line of cobble and boulder and watched a school of black-nosed and rosy-sided dace hold in the pool. Even the fish were there.

I was home. Even though I'd been away for five months, I was comfortable. I could feel the off kilter sensation dissolve as I floated in the moment. I could feel my motivation to enjoy and fight for our rivers return. Streams have been woven into my life. I can't tell my story without including them, and when life gets too busy for me to experience them I feel the effects. I wonder how Basin Run and Deer Creek and all the other rivers I am connected to will change after I haven't been in them for a while, but the biggest shift I notice is in me. Rivers flow. Things change, but there are also constants. Basin Run was there then, and it always will be. But it will be different in the future. Life finds a way. Creek snorkeling helps me remember these truths, and this short dip reconnected, reengaged, re-centered, and re-inspired me to take up the cross of clean water once again.

2. Surprise Encounters

Beavers

Lumps of sawdust-laden beaver poop lay on the bottom, and a fresh beaver chew was placed against what appeared to be an old beaver dam. A pile of pale white sticks glowed from the bottom and were gathered in a tangle along the bank of the creek. The bark was already stripped. I could see a hole in the bank just above the sticks. This was a bank den and I debated about trying to swim in to see if I could spot a beaver. Beaver are portrayed as cute and cuddly loafing animals, but they are huge rodents that can weigh 80 pounds. They are a bit lumbering on land, but are amazingly graceful and agile in the water and they respond aggressively when cornered, like any animal, including humans. I really wanted to see one in its den so I floated above the hole and debated about taking a breath, and a chance, to stick my head into their home.

I suspected this creek was partially beaver controlled, and the fresh signs proved it. Beaver were once one of the most abundant pre- European settlement mammals in North America and there were an estimated two hundred million before the fur trade. They were hunted almost to extinction for their fur and castoreum, a secretion from the scent glands called castor sacs that was used in perfumes and medicine, said to cure headache, fever, and hysteria. The European exploration of North America was largely driven by the exploitation of the beaver, and their population was decimated as a result.

In her book *Water*, Alice Atwater presents a compelling argument about how beaver were responsible for water quality in North America. The ponds formed by beaver dams trap sediment, act as great filters for water, remove nitrogen and phosphorous and create a diversity of habitats. That might explain the greater than expected diversity and abundance of fish seen in Big Branch, which is a small stream. Diverse habitats and clean water supported biologically rich ecosystems. As the beaver were removed, so were the benefits of their engineering. Today they are returning to even urban streams, though we still remove them when they create what we consider flooding problems. Maybe part of the solution to restoring stream health is to leave the beaver alone.

I hovered above the bank den and watched a cloud of small fish enjoy the protection the pile of beaver chew sticks provide. The opening looked big enough for me to get at least my torso into the den and I was tempted to surface dive into the entrance. But there were some unknowns that tempered my drive to explore. Would the opening stay large enough for me to reach an anticipated air pocket on the other side? Would there be a large beaver waiting for me when I surfaced in the den? Or maybe a snapping turtle, or large catfish laying in the aquatic part of the hole? I didn't like the idea of coming face to face with a 50 pound rodent, but took a big breath anyway and submerged. I wasn't sure how long I would have to hold it. I wasn't sure how long the tube was before it curved up above the water line.

The tangle of gnawed sticks at the entrance was thicker than they'd looked from the surface a few feet above. I fought my way through the jumbled branches and started into the entrance. Most of the light was eliminated as soon as my shoulders entered the hole. The tube curved up and narrowed so that both shoulders touched the sides. I had to abort. I backed out, worried I might get hung up in the wood at the entrance. Luckily I slid out easily, and popped to the surface out of breath. It would have been a great experience to see a beaver in its den. Or it might have been a disaster, depending on the beaver's temperament. Either way, I swam on, happy in the knowledge that those large rodents were there, hopeful that I might see one on its own terms, not by invading its space in its den. Happy in the proof that life returns.

Toads

I stood on the bank of the Big Elk and listened to the high trill of the American toad as the sun set. First one called to my right then another answered to my left. A third called from across the stream. It felt early for American Toads to be calling for mates, but here they were, trilling away. I scared one couple, in amplexus, into the water. Amplexus is how toads mate. The smaller male climbs on top of the larger female and tightly grasps her, not letting go until she deposits her fertilized eggs.

American toads are an urban success story. They have figured out how to not only tolerate but actually prosper in the most densely populated areas, even though we aren't sure how. They are killed by dogs, chopped by lawn mowers, squished by cars, and still they thrive. Toads are amphibians, which means they spend part of their lives in water and part on land. Toads move into water to breed, and in urban areas toad accessible water can be scarce. The male fertilizes the female's eggs as she lays them. The eggs hatch in 3-12 days into toad poles, who look like tiny black squiggles. The toad poles sprout legs, absorb their tails, and become toadlets in 50 days, when they hop out of the water.

I wanted to capture images of the toads in amplexus because it is such a sign of hope and an incredible story of amazing nature accessible to everyone. There was only ten minutes of daylight left; by the time I suited up it would be dark, so I decided to come back in two days, when I had more time. I figured the toads would still be there trilling and in amplexus two days from then.

I returned as planned, but the toads were done; their eggs were laid. I should have gotten in the water with the toads when I'd had the chance. Things change fast in a stream. But still I suited up to explore what is a very impacted creek. The Big Elk is a heavily urbanized stream. The bottom is completely embedded in deposited silt so that it's now one continuous sand flat, with no cobble, and therefore, little habitat. Over-fertilized water results in long stringy mustardy tan algae that covers everything.

I slid into the water, disappointed that I'd missed the toads, and thought the trip was a waste. The stream was featureless except for a half-submerged tree trunk, and a tire filled with sand. It was like swimming over a lunar landscape. Barren. But then—life. A white sucker swam for a deeper hole and got used to my presence so that I could watch it without it hustling for cover. Tessellated darters sent up fine puffs of sediment as they shot away. A small school of small sunnies held under the sunken tree. I turned to see if anything was trailing me and saw a large school of common shiners. I had stirred a lot of the string algae off of the bottom into a flocculent cloud, and the shiners fed in it. I got a face full of the olive chunky haze as I turned upstream and really hoped I didn't get any into my snorkel. I tried not to gag, as I thought about the possibility.

I continued to crawl upstream over the plain sand bottom. Then I saw lines of black dots in thin jelly tubes. They looked like small black pearls encased in clear plastic sheaths. Some of the strands were curled around upon themselves, others trailed straight in the downstream current. They were the eggs that would hatch into toadpoles in a few days. These were the next generation of amphibious urban survivors. I might have missed the opportunity to capture toads mating, but I captured images of the next toad generation. There is nothing more hopeful in ecology than reproducing populations, and I felt grateful to be able to witness the process. At times it feels like nature and humans are incompatible. That wherever we go, we push out all that is natural. It is easy to think that nature doesn't exist among us but rather is relegated to the truly great spaces like Yellowstone or Shenandoah. But watching these toads in this urban stream showed me that nature is here too, and it is just as amazing.

Frogs

Just a few degrees make a huge difference, so when temperatures climbed into the 40s it looked, felt, and smelled like spring. It was a prime opportunity to get into one of my favorite creeks to see if things underwater were changing as fast as they seemed to be on land. I was specifically trying to learn the timing of a large darter gathering at a local waterfall. I'd watched them congregate there for the last two years, and wondered if it was just a fluke, or if the meeting was intentional and specifically timed with the season.

The air might have been warm but the water still stung as I climbed in. I'm used to it now, and soon the cold didn't register. There were no darters still and I started to get a little concerned. There had been darters there at the same time the previous year. In fact, they had been there two weeks earlier the previous year, and I'd hoped they'd return. The water temperature was three degrees colder than the year before and maybe that slight difference explained their absence.

I inched my way down a shallow riffle and saw movement out of the corner of my eye. I couldn't make out what splashed into the deeper, faster moving water, but I assumed it was some kind of fish. I slid over algae covered rocks and sailed into a deeper pool with a strong recirculating current.

A frog twirled in the strong eddy, and did slow turns between the surface and sand bar bottom. I thought it was dead, and thought what a waste. I wondered what killed it as I circulated with its motionless body through an eddy. It looked so clean. Its legs were a creamy white and brilliant yellow. Its abdomen looked strong, and its body intact as we twirled together in a kind of a post mortem dance. It lifelessly flew through the water. I reached out, grabbed it, and felt one of its hind legs push slowly but firmly against my hand. The frog wasn't dead. It was cold. Frogs, like other amphibians, are ectotherms which is a more accurate descriptor for animals typically called coldblooded. Their blood isn't necessarily cold. Rather, their body temperature generally matches the temperature of the surrounding environment. So, when it is cold out ectotherems, including frogs, are less active and many hibernate for the winter. When it warms, they get active.

Some frogs must have taken advantage of the warmer day and emerged. The movement I'd seen earlier that I'd assumed to be fish wriggling for deeper water I now thought had been frogs, right on the cusp of the breeding season, wanting to be the first ones out to increase their chances of attracting a mate. The males inflate sacs under their throats to produce calls that attract females. Each species of frog has a distinctive call. This cold frog was probably one of the eager ones.

I placed the frog in a calm shallow pool near the shore, and it assumed the usual frog position, legs under body, poised to jump. Soon this river would be full of darters and trilling frogs, hopefully migrating herring too. The pent up biological energy was almost palpable. We were right on the cusp of spring, and the frogs were flying.

Oddly, I've had more encounters with frogs during winter than I have in warmer weather. They are too fast in summer, I guess. But one winter night I came across an interesting find. I was just about to get out of the freezing water but decided to make one more pass down a short rapid. There on the bottom, wedged nose first under the upstream lip of a cobble, was a frog. Her banded hind legs were drawn up tight under her sides. For a minute I thought she might be dead. What was a frog doing out in barely above-freezing water? Had she been over-wintering here? Seemed like a pretty forceful flow for a frog to overwinter. Maybe the tradeoff was the oxygen-rich water.

The frog's nictitating membranes covered her eyes, so that they glowed zombie white, and I wasn't convinced she was alive. I really didn't want to disturb the frog, but my curiosity won and I gently poked her hind quarters. She tucked tighter into the rock. The frog was definitely alive, and had chosen to spend at least this part of winter here, huddled on the bottom of this rapid. I watched the frog for a while, and tried to get a good photo without disturbing the amphibian any more than I already had. I could see my breath float across the moon as I got out of the water into the cold dark night, exhilarated.

Amphibians in other parts of the world are in trouble. Habitat loss, climate change related disease, insecticide induced mutations are taking their toll. So I'm always appreciative of what I get to watch in our rivers. It's even more profound when what I watch is something as unexpected as frogs in winter.

Turtles

I don't usually snorkel with the intention to observe turtles, but I often find them. One trip to Hildacy Farm resulted in a really important turtle find. Hildacy Farm is the headquarters of the Natural Lands Trust, a nonprofit land conservation organization that protects forests, fields, streams, and wetlands in eastern Pennsylvania and Southern New Jersey. I stopped at Hildacy to snorkel Crum Creek as part of a project to document the amazing underwater life found in the streams protected by the Trust. Crum Creek skirts along the edge of the 55 acre property just downstream of Springton Reservoir. The water looked a little milky and churned up by the outfall below the dam a couple of hundred yards upstream. I wasn't sure if I would see anything.

There wasn't much life there, at least not at first, so I admired the unique asteroid texture of the clay and gravel stream bed. I grappled my way upstream and surveyed the bottom. It was winter and life had wriggled into the bottom and moved to deeper spots, which made it hard to see.

The river carved a three foot hole out of the clay and cobble under a tree root mass. It was dark in the back of this hollow and I almost ignored it. I took a breath, clung to the bottom, and inched my way in. As soon as my eyes adjusted to the low light I saw the large turtle wedged into the bottom. I came up for an excited breath and eased back down to try to get a positive identification and a few pictures. I didn't want to disturb the reptile since I was fairly certain it was hunkered down there for the winter.

The prominent vertical red stripes on its shell confirmed my suspicion that it was a northern red-belly cooter. This was a first for me. I have seen these beautiful animals on the surface but I've never swum with one. I watched from a distance to make sure I didn't interrupt its hibernation. Seeing firsthand where and how a turtle hibernates was incredible. The fact that red-bellied cooters are threatened in Pennsylvania, and federally endangered, made this find even sweeter. Red-bellied numbers have declined due to the loss of habitat to suburban development. It was no coincidence that that red-bellied cooter was there on a Natural Lands Trust preserve.

I left the stream feeling energized and excited for my next exploration of a stream protected by protected land. How we treat land matters. The critically important work of the land preserving organizations protects not only essential terrestrial habitats but aquatic ones too, and I couldn't wait to see what discoveries await in other preserve creeks.

A few months later I was in Big Branch, a stream that runs through a preserve in northeastern Maryland. Large male sunfish took me on as I approached their nests. They flashed neon turquoise stripes and one even turned red. A big school of large fall fish swirled in a hole beneath some big woody debris. A small mouth bass challenged me just like the sunnies, charging at my mask. Swarms of young darters hopped along the sand flats. Mixed schools of rosy-sided dace, black-nosed dace, and common shiner swam upstream in the current past me in lock step order and looked like a group of leaves in the wind as they flowed back downstream in disarray. This was the typical Big Branch. Full of tons of life that display incredible behaviors.

I reached the big pool and started the slow float downstream. I decided to go a little past my usual takeout to explore an oak that had recently fallen into the river. As I approached I thought I saw the shell of a turtle but it could have been a rock or other obstruction sticking out of the mud and sand bottom. Then I saw the head. Sure enough it was a snapper. I've never seen this animal in the water. All of my encounters with snappers have been on land where they are slow and clunky, except for their strike. But in the water this animal is agile and graceful. And just like on land, this animal didn't want anything to do with me. It started to back away as soon as it saw me approach. I kept my distance, not out of fear but rather respect. I'm not afraid of snappers. I don't ascribe to the commonly held belief that these turtles can shear a broomstick in half. I've trapped turtles for five years as part of a mark and recapture program to determine population size and migration patterns, and found them to not be the finger-removing monsters they are made out to be. Rather, they respond like any other animal when threatened and cornered.

Once, while checking traps for the mark recapture study, I found that one of the nets contained two large snappers in addition to a dozen painted turtles. I took all of the painted turtles out of the trap and worked to free the first snapper. The turtle was surprisingly strong, and I had difficulty holding on to its hind legs as I untangled the net from its long dark claws. The turtle unleashed its coiled neck with a lightning fast strike at the air that made its entire 20 pound body jump off the deck. It wasn't even aiming for me, it was a defensive jab and jump at the air. As I focused on freeing this first turtle, I lost track of the second, and felt a strong punch on my right hand. The second turtle was there, and lashed its head at me, mouth closed. I gave this turtle the opportunity to inflict injury, but it didn't take it. I've been hit by the head of a closed-mouthed snapping turtle many times since. It's almost as if they use their head as a warning shot rather than immediately striking with a snapping mouth.

The turtle in the water now was more agile than the ones I'd encountered on land. It was in its aquatic element and started to back up as I approached. I floated and watched the large reptile. Its shell was covered in algae fur, and its starred eyes remained fixed on me. I tried to not get too close, or make abrupt moves because I didn't want to disturb the turtle. But the current had other ideas and I wound up floating too close for the turtle's comfort. It left me alone in the creek with a few graceful flicks of its hind feet.

But turtles don't just inhabit pristine environments. I've seen them in highly altered streams. Jordan Creek runs through Allentown, PA. The creek's banks are walls of concrete, and the river is forced into a thin sheet of water over a low head dam that looks like it also served as a wet crossing for vehicles at one time, since it's about six feet wide. A red-eared slider lay on the bottom of the quiet part of the plunge pool below the dam and craned its neck toward the surface to watch me watch it. Red-eareds are native to the Midwest and are common pet store turtles. This reptile could be a pet that gained its freedom when its keeper got tired of caring for it. Or it could be part of the introduced eastern Pennsylvania population that is now reproducing.

I've also seen turtles in water that wasn't protected by preserved land. The Susquehanna River around Harrisburg is pretty heavily exploited. The land surrounding this part of the river is developed, and numerous dams and power plants use the river to generate power. I got into the river at that point to explore, to experience adventure in a built up setting and to understand that even urban rivers are wild. The bottom is angled bedrock that slants at 45 degrees and is covered in olive algae. There are lots of nooks and crannies for life to hide and I saw small mouth bass and very abundant crayfish. I drifted over an eddy where leaves, twigs, and the shells of dead Asian clams and crayfish had accumulated.

A small turtle looked back. Its saucer-sized body was clean and green with thin yellow lines squiggled over its skin. The lines extended onto its shell, but were less distinct. They looked like the lines on a contour map, which gives this turtle its name: map turtle. I initially got very excited, because I thought it might be a northern map turtle. Northern map turtle populations are likely shrinking due to declining water quality and they are endangered in Maryland, just 40 miles south. It turned out that it was a common map turtle rather than the less abundant and declining Northern map, but that didn't diminish the excitement I felt when I saw that beautiful creature.

I don't see turtles regularly when I snorkel. If they are present in the rivers I explore, they are usually gone long before I know they are there. But seeing them is always a special surprise.

Snakes

A family rushed past me on the trail that leads to Deer Creek. "There's a copperhead down there in the creek bed. I wouldn't go down there." The father says, hurriedly.

"Thanks for the heads up," I said, and continued to the stream as people surged out of a favorite swimming hole, leaving better visibility and more room for me. I knew I wouldn't find a copperhead. It would be a northern water snake.

I don't like snakes. I like to watch them, but I'm not big on handling them. I've been bitten before—always my fault. I've learned that, when you grab one, they tend to grab back. Water snakes are common in our rivers and streams in summer, and every time I see one in the water, I try to swim with it, but usually can't keep up. They really don't want anything to do with us and quickly disappear into the distance. But once in a while I get lucky and see the snake before it sees me and swims away. I'd watched a water snake hunt on the bottom of the Delaware in six feet of water. The bright red, brown, and gray diamond pattern on its body looked like a moving, intricate mosaic. The snake methodically probed under and around rocks looking for fish. I surface dived to the bottom to get a better look and hung on to a rock while I watched the snake hunt. It saw me, startled when it did, and quickly swam away. I was able to keep up for a few feet, but was no match for the aquatic agility of the reptile and it easily escaped my sight.

A few weeks later I was snorkeling a shallow rocky section of the Susquehanna while being interviewed for a story about Susquehanna River snorkeling.

"Snake!" the reporter shouted.

"Where?" I shouted back, about to jump out of the water. I knew better, knew that water snakes are non-aggressive, but memories of getting grabbed back after grabbing them were still fresh.

"Over there. Its head is just behind that rock."

There was a slab of bedrock that separated me from the snake, so I couldn't see it. The reporter guided me in.

"He's right over there, just on the other side of the rock."

I inched around, really hoping it would be long gone as part of me didn't want to come face to face with a water snake. But I had to prove to this writer that water snakes really were non-aggressive, so I pressed on.

I cautiously peeked around the rock. Nothing but crayfish.

"He took off. Its way over there." The reporter pointed across the river bed, proving my point about the snake being non-aggressive.

The next summer I saw what looked like a stick poking out of the surface while snorkeling on the Octoraro Creek. I quietly slid into the water and slowly crept closer with the water line in the middle of my mask so I could see above and below the surface on the hunch that it was a water snake. I was right. At about 20 feet I could make out the reptile's round eyes set against a reddish brown head. The snake wasn't sure what to make of me, and its tongue started to flick more frequently when I got to within ten feet. Snakes sense their environments with their tongues and this response let me know the snake knew I was close. I stopped moving toward him and just watched. He was stunning, and I still can't comprehend how anyone could kill these animals out of pure ignorance. They are incredibly striking animals, graceful and adept in the water, and fast on land. Unfortunately, they are constantly confused with the poisonous copperhead. Water snakes aren't poisonous and won't come after people. Their diet is almost entirely fish and it's really amazing to watch them hunt and successfully snag a fish that is often surprisingly large for the snake's body size.

But still, they are regularly the target of rocks thrown by people who just don't understand how harmless they are or how important they are to the stream system. Maybe they just can't see past their unfounded fear to notice the beauty and agility of these extraordinary reptiles.

Leaves

Leaves twirled in the current like feathers in a breeze. Most of them had dropped off trees about a week prior and they populated Deer Creek. I felt like a kid running through blowing swirls of leaves as I hung on to a rock in the rapid and leaves whizzed past. Some got plastered to my snorkel and mask.

A little further upstream, in a more quiet pool, I swam through a snowstorm of sycamore seeds. The frilly tufts that carried them through the air also kept them suspended in the water and they swirled about like snowflakes. There was a collection of walnuts behind a rock in a small rapid.

This was half of the life blood of the stream. The organic inputs from the adjacent forest in the form of leaves, seeds, and twigs provide energy that's converted from plant to animal by a diverse group of insects who shred and ingest the dead leaves. The insects are in turn food for fish. The rest of the stream's energy comes from algae. What I watched was more than just a few leaves twirling in water. I watched an ecological process finely tuned by eons of adaptation. It's part of an interplay of energy between the forest and the stream. In the fall the net energy flow is downstream with the water. In spring and summer, the stream gives energy back to the forest in the form of hatching insects and migrating fish. Some leaves get stuck to rocks or are captured by sprigs of rock weed as they travel by. Others become waterlogged and gather in eddies on the bottom. I was more than watching a process. I was experiencing it. Another leaf plastered itself to my mask.

There aren't many creek snorkeling trips where I don't witness the intimate relationship between leaves and streams. They end up on the bottom, out of the current between stones, or pinned by the current to the upstream sides of rocks. But either way, leaves are an incredibly important source of energy for our stream ecosystems and constitute a large part of the foundation of the creek food web.

Many aquatic insects eat only leaves that fall into creeks. They even have preferences for different tree species. Leaves with higher nitrogen content are usually eaten first; those with lower nitrogen and higher lignin, an organic polymer that forms cell walls in wood bark and leaves, are consumed later in the season. Do the higher nitrogen content leaves taste better to the leaf shredding community of may, caddis, and stone fly? Or are the higher nitrogen and lower lignin leaves consumed first because the high lignin content leaves will last longer in the water, and somehow mayflies, stoneflies, and caddis flies know this? Maybe they eat the leaves that will decompose the fastest first, so there will be food stores in the stream to last through the winter. Or maybe bacteria and fungi need to process the hard to digest lignin before it can be consumed by the creek shredders.

This is just another case of ecological complexity that infers an intelligence at work that we can't comprehend or interpret. Either way, leaves fuel the aquatic insect community, and the aquatic insect community in turn fuels the fish, bird, and bat communities that eat the insects, and so on. This is one of the reasons why our creeks need to have forests lining their shores—streams need leaves to fuel their food webs, and forests need creeks to fuel theirs. Trees play other important roles in creek ecology. They provide shade, which keeps creek waters cool. Their roots hold soil in place and reduce the amount of gill-choking sediment entering the water. Nitrogen and Phosphorous are nutrients that make plants grow. When excess nitrogen and phosphorous get into water they make too much algae grow. Algae doesn't live for long and when it dies, bacteria use up oxygen as they decompose the dead algae. This results in oxygen poor water that can't support life, and this process is called eutrophication. Trees filter excess nitrogen and phosphorous from runoff, which prevents eutrophication. One of the simplest things we can do for stream restoration is plant trees.

Even in summer, when the forest canopy is full and leaves are still firmly attached to their twigs, leaves enter creeks and flow downstream until they become waterlogged or lodged somewhere. In the fall when the canopy drops, large flocculent aggregations of yellow, orange and brown leaves fill the bottoms of the deeper holes and make the bottom look like a multicolored decoupage. The life on the bottom of the creek takes advantage of the new cover and food. It's hard for me to snorkel over leaf mats on the bottom of slower sections of streams without stirring up at least one northern hog sucker, a half dozen tessellated darters, and a bunch of crayfish. So the forest fuels the stream, but we are learning that the stream fuels the forest in return.

Dr. Mary Power, a professor at UC Berkeley, observed that spider webs were much larger further from the stream compared to the webs close to the stream, and reasoned that the cause was that more emerging insects close to the stream meant those spiders didn't need to invest as much energy in web construction since food was abundant. Compared to spiders in more interior parts of the forest, which had to build more elaborate webs to capture the same quantity of food. She tested her theory by trapping insects at varying distances from the stream, and estimated that 96% of all emerging insects become part of the forest ecosystem.

We draw a line between wet and dry, terrestrial and aquatic. But when we look at energy flow there's no divider. What we do on land affects the water, and water quality affects land based systems. Terrestrial, aquatic, and human are intimately connected. The boundaries between them are artificial constructions we create.

Algae

Algae covered all of the rocks and waved in the current like fine brownish green hair. It hadn't been in Basin Run two weeks ago, and in just this short time, it had covered everything. My heart sank. Could I have caused this? Was I responsible for bringing algae from one stream to another? The rocks had been clean when I'd snorkeled Basin Run two weeks earlier.

Algae isn't bad in moderation. In fact it's essential. Stream ecosystems are fueled through two main routes: inputs from the surrounding land (ideally in the form of leaf fall and terrestrial insects), and through the food produced by the photosynthesizing biofilm that covers just about every non-living thing in the stream. Biofilms are communities of tiny organisms such as bacteria, diatoms, and other kinds of algae, that serve critical functions in streams, in addition to producing much of the food needed by the organisms who live there. Biofilms are responsible for the cycling and transformation of nitrogen, phosphorous, and carbon, nutrients essential to the health of the stream. They also create dramatic underwater stream-scapes and significantly add to the beauty and otherworldly mysterious feel of many of the streams I snorkel. Algae are normal and needed, but too much algae, or the wrong kinds, can kill a creek.

A stream in a neighboring county is being taken over by an algal diatom called Didymo. Originally from Scotland, extreme northern Europe, and Asia, Didymo was introduced to the Gunpowder and now has the potential to spread via fly fishers' waders. Its common name—rock snot—accurately describes what it does to creeks. I clean, disinfect and dry my gear as best I can between streams, but still I was afraid I'd biologically contaminated Basin Run by introducing algal hitchhikers riding on my wet suit to the stream. I wouldn't love Basin Run, or any of the other streams I snorkel, any less if they were to become more degraded than they are. But I don't want to be the one contributing to that degradation. I don't have the right to degrade the homes of the stream dwelling organisms I take so much pleasure in watching.

I visited a stream 20 minutes from my house to see if algae covered everything there, and I checked Basin Run, well upstream from my usual snorkeling spot, the site where I might have introduced some algal invaders. I was relieved to find the same kind of thick algal covering in places where I'd never snorkeled. Most likely the sudden growth of algae in Basin Run is a normal seasonal change. Part of the seasonal progression streams experience that I am just starting to understand, and like everything else in the stream, is probably related to seasonal changes in the forest. The leaves have fallen from the canopy, which allows more sunlight to reach the stream. Since algae need sunlight to grow, this could result in more algae. Leaves add nutrients to the stream and can make algae grow as, like any other plant, algae need nitrogen and phosphorous to grow. Grazers, those organisms like snails, and certain kinds of mayfly, stonefly, and caddis fly larvae, who eat algae, aren't as active when the water cools, so the algae can grow unchecked. Maybe the change in growth is a seasonal shift in the biofilm from single celled diatoms, with silica shells, to blue green algae to green algae. This seasonal successional pattern of biofilm composition has been found in other streams, but it is hard to generalize. Each stream is unique. Or maybe it's a combination of all of the above. I've learned through my exploration of rivers and streams not to become alarmed when our rivers turn furry in the fall, even when the change is abrupt.

We are familiar with the terrestrial passage of the seasons, and maybe take how life responds to changes in sunlight intensity, which affects temperatures, for granted. It's a more pronounced change in our streams because we don't live there. Even though streams are familiar, their underwater views are foreign, so changes appear less subtle, more dramatic, and more easily noticed. What most people don't recognize, and I often forget, is that streams have seasons too.

Time goes on, and seasons come and go, even in our rivers and streams. I feel fortunate to watch the underwater seasons pass, generally in step with and definitely linked to the terrestrial ones, which ultimately are affected by cosmic events. But the underwater seasons of our rivers and streams are unique in how they present, and I get to witness the otherworldly seasonal progression.

Part of that progression is in summer, when days are long and the water is warm and grazers keep the algae in check. On this day, I heard the faint clicking intensify as a school of them approached. Then the bottom of the river, downstream of where I lay, started to wriggle, and I realized that the stonerollers had arrived beneath me. They moved across the bottom in a crazed grazing frenzy. Hundreds of them in the same school swam along the bottom, scraping algae from rocks as they moved upstream. Their sides flashed silver with every twisting bite they gouged from the algae that covered rocks and their jaws snapped, which explained the clicking sound.

Stonerollers are some of my favorite fish, partly because of the elaborate stone piling mating rituals the males use to attract females in the spring. But I also like them because they are really a non-descript fish for most of the year. However, careful observation reveals how well adapted they are for keeping algae in check in our rivers and streams, and the non-descript, even unnoticeable, become incredible.

Their mouths slightly protrude downward, and hard bony plates on their upper jaw leave u-shaped scrapes in rock-coating algae. Dr. Mary Powers, a leading stream ecologist and professor at UC Berkeley, conducted an interesting exclusion experiment with stonerollers. Bass are stoneroller predators, so she excluded stonerollers from sections of river by keeping bass there, and eliminated bass from other sections. The sections where the bass were kept became overgrown in algae. This demonstrates the importance of the stonerollers to the system, but it also illustrates the often unnoticed, and hidden, interrelationships between everything in nature. Everything matters and as naturalist and early advocate of wilderness preservation John Muir said, "When we try to pick out anything by itself, we find it hitched to everything else in the universe." Algae, bass, and marauding stonerollers.

There's joy in watching this eons old progression as our streams change almost daily, and participating in the process of exploration—discovering the intimate interplay between terrestrial and aquatic such that the lines distinguishing them blur. It really is just one system, and it's all related, us included. Which is why all of our actions, even those we perceive to be benign, have an effect—positive or negative.

Hellbenders

I got a text from Jeremy Monroe, Director of Freshwaters Illustrated, a non-profit dedicated to bringing the underwater world of our rivers and streams to light through video, saying that the Tellico River just behind the cabin I was staying in held hellbenders. Southeastern U.S. rivers are home to some of the most diverse freshwater biology in the world. Freshwaters Illustrated was there to document that diversity. I was there as part of my efforts to develop curriculum to accompany Freshwaters Illustrated films. Seeing a hellbender on this trip would be phenomenal. Hellbenders are foot long salamanders, giants in North American terms. They need cold, clean water to survive so their numbers are declining and their range is shrinking, since cold clear streams are becoming rare. I've never seen one, even though I've been on an unofficial search for the last five years, looking for them any time I'm in their range. I want to see one in case they disappear from the wild, but I have hope that we can protect the populations that remain.

Hellbenders are important to me because they represent wild rivers. They are a species that was present where I live, that are now thought to be gone because of increased sediments that come from the things we do on land, and because some fishermen killed the ones they caught. Even today they are found dead wrapped in fishing line on rivers in the southern Appalachians. I would like to think that there are still hellbenders in the lower Susquehanna. The large slabs of bedrock habitat is perfect for them, and is part of the reason for my hope that a population is still hiding somewhere in the nine mile stretch of river below the Conowingo Dam. Even if the lower Susquehanna hellbenders are gone, I believe that maybe they can be restored. This is why I want to find them in the Tellico River in Tennessee.

Dave Herasimtschuk, a photographer/videographer with Freshwaters Illustrated, saw a half dozen hellbender out in the open at the same spot a month ago when waters were much colder. The search was on. Jeremy Monroe, Dave Herasimtschuk, Casper Cox, and I slipped into the river and searched for two hours before dusk.

The Tellico is interesting. I searched through three feet deep smooth-walled canyons the water had carved from the otherwise jagged bedrock. I dived to the bottom to peer into the shadows formed under the ledges of larger rocks, which is typical hellbender habitat, and I looked in the small crannies of the fractured bedrock, which isn't. Orange and black striped tangerine darters were plentiful, and they put on colorful displays that made not finding any hellbenders okay.

We conjectured why we hadn't seen any hellbenders since they'd been so abundant a month ago, and figured that water temperatures had gone up. So either the hellbenders had headed upstream to cooler waters, or had assumed their typical secretive, nocturnal habit. They respire through their skin, so water conditions are pretty critical, which is one of the reasons they are at risk. They are very susceptible to low oxygen levels and high sediment loads, and can't tolerate either. Cold water can hold more oxygen than warm water, so we thought they'd either headed upstream for cooler waters, or were active at night since water temps mirror air temperatures slightly and drop after dark. We decided that a night snorkel in the Tellico might help us find one.

It was a few minutes before midnight when I slipped into the dark water. I debated a bit before getting wet, but decided I had to make the attempt to find a hellbender. The water feels bigger at night. The deepest spot on that section of Tellico could have been three feet deep, but it felt like 30 since my sight was limited to a narrow cone of light. I couldn't see more than the reach of the beam which only felt like three feet. I slowly crept upstream through canyons carved through the bedrock, holding on tight to the online search image of a dark brown foot long salamander with a broad mouth and wrinkly folds of skin.

I found a hog sucker that seemed to be sleeping, or dazed by the light and it let me get in close for some photos. A few large red horse startled me as they rocketed out of the dark. I turned to try to get a picture, and one of them hit my thigh hard in the chaos a bright beam of light created in a narrow, deep section all silted up from the commotion. I tried to systematically search by traversing across the river, moving upstream a few feet and coming back. The dark deep canyons were a little unnerving and at times I felt like I was floating in space—dark, cold space. I didn't find any hellbenders and my frustration grew. I started to really question whether I would ever see one in the wild before it was too late.

Two years later, I had an opportunity to snorkel in Pisgah National Forest, North Carolina. National Forest streams are usually excellent places to snorkel due to their forested watersheds, and I looked forward to the trip. But I wasn't thinking about looking for hellbender until I heard they were extremely abundant here. Someone who had snorkeled the river had said they saw six hanging out right in the open that summer, right where I was.

The river was clear and loaded with fish, but that didn't matter. I had a search image of a flattened, round, well camouflaged, mottled head of a salamander blazing in my brain and nothing else mattered. I envisioned it barely peeking out from under a flat rock and I searched for an image to match the one in my head. I was sure I missed some fish. I saw movement in my periphery and dismissed it. It wasn't until I looked to my left and saw a large brown trout holding under a log that I realized I was missing incredible biology for the search of what might be. I was missing what was in front of me, which was pretty awesome, in the quest for something better.

The fish was large as trout go, and beautifully colored with yellow fins and belly, red and brown spots above, and a slightly hooked lower jaw. The large fish just held under the log at the base of a small falls and watched me watch it until it decided I was too much threat to tolerate, then it disappeared with one flick of its tail.

Brown trout are not native to North America. They were brought here from Europe and like the also non-native rainbow trout, are raised in hatcheries and released in our rivers and streams. They are top predators in the aquatic food web, and part of me wonders if the decline we are seeing in hellbender could be related to these non-native fish feeding on hellbender larvae. But this trout was an incredible animal and I shared a similar thrill in watching the brown trout that fly fishers do when they capture this elusive fish.

It definitely would have been amazing to see a hellbender. These animals are so secretive and well camouflaged, and the rivers in Pisgah afford so many places where a hellbender can effectively hide from a snorkeler, I bet that my search was very incomplete, that I was just at Pisgah at the wrong time of year and if I returned in their breeding season, I'd see one. Still, every time I search and come up empty, part of me worries that their numbers are dropping and maybe I'll miss my chance to observe them in the wild, but I'm not done looking. I'll keep peeking under ledges when I snorkel the lower Susquehanna at home. And I will be back to southeastern rivers again to look for those incredible animals. I will continue the search, and keep hope for their survival and restoration.

Lamprey

I'd been lucky enough to take more than one hundred kids snorkeling on rivers on three of the last seven days. It is fun work, but exhausting when done right. I enjoyed the sunny morning and clear water of our last trip. It was the last group of 25 and we had just found about a dozen elvers making their way back upstream to find a clean gravel/cobble bar home where they would mature for the next 25 years or so. It is so rewarding to see kids watch this amazing feat, to watch them become connected to our rivers right before my eyes. The school's principal was also out with this

5th grade class, and she gave an approving nod. We were reaching curricular outcomes. Kids were learning while they explored their river.

I rolled onto my back and enjoyed the rush of water, the sun, the laughter of students. Life was good, and I was satisfied. A commotion downstream changed all that. A half dozen students gathered around a section of riffle and yelled "Eel!" I rolled over and snorkeled to them to find a large, three foot long orange colored lamprey firmly attached to a rock.

I had never seen a lamprey in the wild before. Just as I thought the day couldn't get any better, I saw a life list fish. Some people collect bird life lists. I collect fish, and this was quite the find. I had been hoping to see a lamprey for 20 years. I had been intently searching for five.

Sea lamprey have a reputation of being an invasive parasite that's killing off the Great Lakes' fish populations, which they are, but in Maryland they are native, and declining in number. We think. They really haven't been all that well studied, and historic population data is scarce.

They are a very primitive fish. They even predate sharks. They are so primitive, jaws evolved after lamprey so they are called jawless fish. Instead, they have a sucker disc lined with sharp raspy teeth, which allows them to latch on to the sides of larger fish and suck body fluids to the point of death. While they appear to be a parasite, they are actually a predatory fish since parasites don't typically kill their hosts. They spend their lives at sea and migrate into our rivers and streams to spawn and, like most migratory fish, they are in trouble.

There are few surveys of lamprey where I live, and we don't have a good assessment of lamprey population trends. It is likely that numbers of these fish are dropping like other aquatic migrants such as shad, eels, and sturgeon, due to dams and declining water quality. Freshwaters Illustrated produced an excellent movie about Pacific lamprey called *Lost Fish*. It's a story about the connection native people have with these fish, and their efforts to protect and restore Pacific lamprey. While this is a different species, the story of decline is similar. *Lost Fish* is a story about passion for our natural world.

Elmer Crow was part of the Nez Perce tribe and worked tirelessly to restore Pacific lamprey. I've never met Elmer Crow, but I felt like I knew him after watching *Lost Fish*. What Elmer says in the film resonates with me:

"We are the circle. That's what life is about. We take care of one another. So when we have someone in trouble, that's when the rest of us have to step in."

Elmer saw what he thought was the last Pacific lamprey on the South Fork of the Salmon River in 1974. He was puzzled as to why the Creator showed him this one fish swimming over a sand flat, and he worried that he might have seen the last one. So he dedicated himself to preserving Pacific lamprey. Elmer died in 2013 and I wish I could have had the opportunity to meet him in person.

That day with the students, I watched the lamprey in the water for as long as I could without losing the class. The caramel brown fish clung to a rock with its sucker disc mouth. Its eyes were set back on its head and watched me as I watched it. There was a consciousness in that eye, a kind of ancient wisdom. Its spiracles, precursors to the gills on more evolutionarily modern fish, pumped water. Its nose was beaten and white due to its incredible journey from the sea to this stream.

Maybe it was the look of the fish and its prehistoric place in the evolutionary ladder. Maybe it was its calm demeanor. Even though it was surrounded by 50 students, it just held on to that one rock. Maybe it was the knowledge that its life was almost over after its incredible reproductive journey. Or maybe it was the feeling that I might have been looking at the last one in the Octoraro, just like Elmer experienced in the South Fork in 1974. Maybe it was all of those things, but whatever it was, something instantly bonded me to that lamprey. Like Elmer, I felt a connection to that one fish.

We took lots of pictures and some video and showed the fish to all the kids. In that instant the students became strongly attached to their river and that fish. The lamprey was the galvanizing agent.

As amazing as that fish is, they seem to be forgotten in the east. I hope we can learn how East Coast lamprey are faring, and take action to protect these primitive wonders. I try to tell people about these amazing ancient fish, and the other aquatic migrants who are declining in number every chance I get. But most importantly, I try to share a little of Elmer's passion in the hopes that it will inspire others.

Mussels

I drifted out from the bank into the big open water of the Susquehanna. Conowingo Dam wasn't running, so the water was low and it was easy for me to drift away from the shore without getting swept downstream. There was supposed to be an incredible mussel bed in the area somewhere. I instantly saw thousands of Asian clam shells, an invasive species imported to North America when Chinese immigrants came to build our railroads. The clams have marched across this, and every other temperate continent, and some call this animal the most invasive freshwater organism on the planet. A few more feet out and I started to see dead mussel shells, patina green on white with mother of pearl spots where the adductor mussels attached when the animal was alive. I was hoping to find some live ones.

A shell caught my attention. I stopped, spun around to head up into the current, and swam against the flow. Sure enough, tucked halfway into the sand was a young eastern elliptio mussel. This was a great find. While eastern elliptio mussels aren't endangered, there aren't many young entering the population of the Susquehanna River, especially upstream of the Conowingo Dam.

A population that isn't recruiting or producing new members is destined to collapse, so it seems just a matter of time before elliptios disappear from the Susquehanna. We haven't seen a population decline yet; we think because elliptios are very long lived so the death of the old timers hasn't quite caught up with the lack of young to effect the number of mussels. We think there are few elliptio mussels being produced because juvenile eels can't make it past Conowingo on their upstream return to the river, and eels, we think, are essential to elliptio reproduction.

Many mussel species depend on fish for reproduction. Some mussel species can only use a particular species of fish. Elliptios aren't as picky, but are largely, not entirely, dependent on American eels. The female elliptio produces glochidia and spits a spider web of them into the water and substrate. Glochidia are juvenile mussels, that aren't quite in adult form. They need to go through a metamorphosis before they assume the final shape of a small mussel. The glochidia latch on to the eels when they pass through the web and start their lives as parasites. While attached, the glochidia undergo a transformation and start to resemble small mussels. After four weeks, the glochidia drop from the eels and settle into the bottom of the river as baby elliptios where they will live, possibly for the next one hundred years. Knowing the complex and intricate reproductive biology behind this juvenile makes me appreciate its presence that much more.

Freshwater mussels as a class are one of the most imperiled groups of North American freshwater organisms, and species besides eastern elliptios have declined throughout North America. Seventy percent of the 297 species are considered vulnerable, imperiled, or already extinct. Causes include damming rivers, sedimentation, and introduced species.

While seeing a juvenile mussel was a hopeful sign, it's only one mussel, and I continued to search. The bottom was just cobble and sand, and nothing popped out. I decided to start to follow a more intentional search pattern and zig-zagged back and forth across the current, slowly making my way upstream with each pass. Finally, I saw the frills and open slit of an incurrent syphon. Then another and another. I was finally on the bed. There were hundreds of adult mussels there, all filtering.

Mussels do a great job of blending in so most people don't know they are there, and most people don't realize their water filtering abilities. Mussels are filter feeders. They pull water in through their incurrent syphon, filter out particles from the water, including algae and sediment, and return cleaner water to the river through their excurrent syphon. They extract food morsels from all of the retained particles and secrete the rest to the bottom. They are even capable of capturing and destroying viruses.

Bill Lellis a biologist from the U.S. Geologic Survey researched the filtering capacity of the elliptio population in the Delaware River and found that they filter between two and six billion gallons of water per day. I have a hard time conceptualizing two to six billion so just as a point of reference, Baltimore City "only" uses about 50 million gallons per day. Freshwater mussels can do the heavy lifting of water filtration and, therefore, water quality improvement.

I've seen the impressive mussel beds Bill Lellis and his team counted during their research. I floated on the surface in six feet of water on the Upper Delaware, while leading a trip with students. Piles of dead shell had accumulated behind larger rocks where the current had dropped them, but I needed live ones. I needed to find life to keep the students I was guiding engaged. Once again, just as I thought the search was for naught, I saw one mussel, with its shell agape, frilled syphons in action, and soon a vast prairie of mussels came into view. The students were instantly amazed at the extent of the bed and the mosaic of metallic indigo, sky blue, and peach their shells and syphons formed.

I've also seen mussels in the most unexpected places. The Upper Delaware is a clean healthy river compared to the lower Brandywine, but I have found mussels even in this impaired waterway. Signs warn fishermen to not consume too much fish caught out of a stretch of the Brandywine just north of Wilmington, because they are contaminated. The Brandywine's industrial past lingers today, and based on the signs, I didn't expect to see anything that might remotely need decent water quality to survive.

I drifted down river in the gentle current and enjoyed watching small mouth bass and darters. Something caught my eye. It looked like a mussel shell, but that wasn't possible. Not in that degraded urban water. I tried to find it again, but couldn't. I assumed it was a leaf and continued downstream. But then the faintest of straight lines emerged from the bottom, and then another and a dozen more. The straight lines were all freshwater mussel shell openings, and I realized I was swimming over a mussel bed. I hovered over the bed until I started to shiver.

The fact that the future of these mussels is uncertain made me appreciate their presence more. But the alive, vibrant mussel beds also gave me hope for their continued existence, and I wanted to savor the feeling of optimism.

Worlds, Rocked

What seem like small perturbations become world changing events down at the scale of our stream-dwelling neighbors. I've learned that I can cause those world changing events just with my presence. Caddisflies, like many aquatic insects, spend the majority of their lives as juveniles under water. They emerge as adults, often en masse, and their emergence is one of the greatest events in nature. I've been on the Susquehanna River on July nights in the middle of these hatches and could hardly see, the flies were so thick. Once emerged, the adults don't eat. They mate, the females lay eggs, and they die.

Caddisflies, along with other bottom dwelling insects like stone and mayflies are the building blocks of healthy stream ecosystems, and are eaten by just about any creek dwelling fish. Most caddisfly larvae build intricate homes out of small bits of stone, sticks, or other plant matter. But hydropsyche caddisflies build webs that harvest organic particles from the current. Some species construct great ballooning socks. The open ends face upstream and the inch or so long sack trails behind in the current and catches whatever floats in. The larval caddisfly then eats the edible bits that are trapped.

While floating in a foot and a half of water, amazed at the abundance of webs stretched between rocks in a section of stream that at first glance appeared lifeless, I noticed one of these larger socks nestled into a shallow crevasse between a few rocks, out of the direct hard current that would have probably shredded the net, but in just enough flow to keep it inflated and catching for the caddisfly. How hydropsyche caddisflies know where to construct their webs in just the right places with just the right flow conditions is beyond me, and indicates a degree of intelligence humans don't possess.

As I floated on the surface, my body changed the hydraulics in that section of stream,
and forced great currents of water to the bottom, great for hydropsyche caddisfly webs. But, while I couldn't feel any difference in water velocity, it was obviously a more significant flow for the web. The intricately constructed sock waved violently in the strong current. It flattened to the bottom and widely expanded and quivered, but withstood the force until I could orient my body so that I didn't interfere nearly as much with the flow of water passing through the web. What seemed like such an insignificant change in water flow to me posed a very significant threat to the caddisfly who occupied that particular web.

I've learned that I can always count on caddisflies to be present in the streams I snorkel, even in the middle of winter. One trip in particular taught me this. The water at Deer Creek, a tributary to the lower Susquehanna, was a lot colder than I expected and I wondered if the effort to get into a dry suit was worth it. I doubted I'd see any fish as cold as the water felt. But Deer Creek was clear and I'm always grateful for good visibility, so I slid into the rapid.

At first there didn't seem to be much life. The usual rock weed covered the boulders, but looked thinner and drab compared to summer. It looked likes the rocks were balding. I didn't see any non-plant life, as the water stung the exposed skin on my face. I swam out into the fast flow and clawed upstream, into a familiar eddy behind a large familiar rock. This is where I go for short quick snorkels, when I just need to get in a river.

Smooth cylinders started to emerge on the face of the large boulder that forced the river flow to divide. Humpless caddisflies live in these smooth cylinders, which they construct, and extend their legs up into the current, to filter morsels of food from the water as it rushes by. Here, they quaked in the strong current, and my placement in the river changed the current dramatically for these small insects. Other caddisflies clung to algae threads on rocks.

I drifted out of the slower eddy, and crept into the strong current where I was whisked downstream. I snagged a rock edge with one hand and let my floating body trail behind. I felt free. I slowly crawled upstream against the strong water, and noticed that there were hundreds, possibly thousands, of caddis cases all facing up into the current, all with black legs stretched into the current, feeding.

This is how I usually see caddis—in their larval, aquatic cased forms. But once I was fortunate enough to witness adult caddis laying eggs.

Deer Creek runs clear through a rapid I snorkel regularly. As soon as I put my face in this familiar spot, a very foreign stream-scape appeared. For as many times as I've been here, this was new. Algae covered the rock moss carpet in pinks and orange pastels, and silver dots crawled down the lee face of a large rock in a rapid.

The silver dots were caddisflies and they glowed as they crawled down the front of a rock back into the rapid. I thought they might be recently metamorphosed adults, emerging, and tried to get some close up photos to document this phenomenon. But I wasn't sure what these flies were doing—coming or going. Adult caddis flitted just above the surface in clumsy flight. But as I watched those silver-coated adults slowly creep back into this rapid, I realized that the silver was from an envelope of air that surrounded the adult caddis flies body. A bubble of air was trapped on the fine hairs that cover the insects' bodies. These were mated females returning to the water to lay their eggs to ensure the next generation; their last act before their death.

Caddis are always in creeks, and in just about every creek I snorkel. I'm used to them and I thought I knew their biology. But that day changed all that. I'd never witnessed adult caddis walking back into the water shrouded by a quicksilver layer of air. I never expected it. I'd learned the caddis life cycle in ecology. I'd learned that the females lay eggs after they mate, but no one had ever told what that looked like. No one had ever told me what an amazing sight it was to watch adult caddisflies return to the water encased in silver bubbles of air to lay their eggs. Maybe the professors who had taught me didn't know. Maybe they'd never witnessed the caddis return to water.

It's a shame, because if more people knew about the miracles taking place in our creeks and rivers, maybe they would care more. Not just knowledge of the mechanics of the process, but rather what the process actually looks like, and how it feels to be a part of it, being a direct witness and to ask questions like, "Why are there silver caddisflies walking down this rock?" Maybe then people would care more for our most vital resource—water—and maybe then more people would feel alive by experiencing the excitement of discovery.

3. Impacts

Life Finds a Way

I knelt in the two foot deep water of Laurel Hill Creek in Southwestern Pennsylvania and clouds of silt swirled from the bottom. The July temperatures meant that wearing a wet suit in this shallow, warm creek was thermal overkill, but I wished I had one on, at least to give me the impression of separation from what appeared to be a dead stream. Route 31 was to my back and I could hear the traffic bang across the bridge. I reluctantly put my masked face into the water and took a few hard breaths as I adjusted to the water temperature and stark view.

    The traffic noise was replaced with the sound of my breath rushing through my snorkel. Fine sickly grayish brown silt enveloped the bottom. The water was clear, but there was no life. Not even the usual thin algal mat that covers everything in many of the streams I've visited. The algal growth is a sign of eutrophication. Ecosystems, especially aquatic ones, need algae, which form the foundation of food webs. But too much algae create an unhealthy system. Algae are essentially a kind of plant. They are different, of course, since they have a hold fast or attachment point instead of roots, but they serve similar purposes. They produce food that fuels the rest of the ecosystem. They need nutrients, specifically nitrogen and phosphorous, to grow. Too much nitrogen and phosphorous means too much algae. Most algae are short lived and when they die, they rob oxygen from the water as they decompose, which results in water that can't support much life. The excess nitrogen and phosphorous come from us in the form of sewage, lawn fertilizer, farm fertilizer, and car exhaust. Everything we do on land and in the air affects freshwater systems, and we are over-fertilizing most of them on the planet, which causes widespread eutrophic conditions.

    But Laurel Hill Creek didn't even have that eutrophic algal mat growing in it. I crawled my way upstream along the bottom in a foot of water. Rock masses formed otherworldly shapes in this lifeless realm. No fish. I thought that I would at least see a sucker. Why was the rural stream in such a degraded state? I picked up a small rock and found a young crayfish. At least the stream wasn't completely devoid of life. The small crustacean took its time backing into its hole. A large, disjointed, dead crayfish claw lay near the base of another stone. Rock, apparently imported to this stream for some construction project (maybe the route 31 bridge), littered the bottom. It didn't fit with the native geology, and gave the place a very strange, artificial feel. A pipeline marker loomed out of the four foot murk. This stream was obviously harshly used. Its bottom had been torn up and replaced with alien material. Its water was unnaturally hot. Excess algae grew from excess nutrients. In total, it was Mars. Finally, I came upon a mass of brilliant green filamentous algae that rested like a large wad of green cotton on a rock. At least there was some kind of life in this Martian desert

    I returned to the stream later that night as lightning flashed in the distance, with the hunch that Laurel Hill Creek is loaded with crayfish. I was right. As soon as my light hit the water, dozens of pairs of orange reflecting crayfish eyes shone back. Laurel Hill Creek isn't all dead. There is life there, and the life in Laurel Hill Creek is just as fascinating as the life in a more pristine creek. But the question of why Laurel Hill is degraded remains, which will lead to the important answer of what can be done to reverse the damage.

Often, I find that even degraded streams retain a certain beauty and mystery that inspires exploration. One of those streams is the little North East. It turns from a piedmont stream, with lots of riffle and run sections, to a coastal plain stream with a relatively gentle flow due to flat geography and a sandy rather than rocky bottom, right about where it crosses under Route 40. That section of the stream was completely dug up for a sewer line to pass under the creek bed to a new pump station on the creek's northern bank two years ago.

I slipped into the shallow water below the Route 40 bridge, and saw a large expanse of algae-covered sand flat. There weren't any fish here. No crayfish. No obvious life except for the algal mat, not even any relief from the monotonous bottom, except for the few sandbag remnants of a coffer dam constructed for the sewer line routing effort. A large rimless truck tire loomed out of the distance, half buried in the sand. The continuous loud high-pitched whine of a pump droned in the background, and gave the place an eerie industrial feel. I've read accident reports that involved divers drowning after being trapped against water intakes, and while I was fairly certain this was the site of a pumping station and not a water intake, I was still nervous.

The sandy bottom sloped off to a three foot deep hole with tree trunks and branches lodged against an old stump in the steeply cut bank. A school of pumpkinseed sunfish gathered near the wood. I was fairly certain I'd seen the shadow of a small mouth bass swim off, and a calico-colored hog sucker darted from the gravel bottom just as I passed over it, much like a stingray glides over the sand with one powerful flick of its wings. The stream was far from dead, and witnessing those fish lessened the industrial feel. Stringy brown strands of algae waved toward the surface as oxygen bubbles suspended them in the water. Even that sign of a degraded stream had a certain beauty about it, and part of its attraction was that life could find a way in that used stream.

Another heavily used stream is Mill Creek, and the odor of detergent was strong long before I saw the stream. Sewage treatment plants are pretty good at removing disease causing organisms and the organic matter that is contained in sewage, but most treatment plants don't have nutrient reducing technology and so they don't do much to lessen the nutrient load entering streams. Too many nutrients makes too much algae grow. Too much algae robs water of oxygen and limits the kind and numbers of fish that can survive there. They also don't do much to reduce the smell of laundry detergent. At least in my experience, the smell of laundry detergent is characteristic of all sewage treatment plant effluent I have encountered.

Mill Creek is a tiny stream that flows through the tiny town of Perryville, and Perryville discharges its treated sewage into Mill Creek. Mill Creek is one of these anomaly streams. It lies in the coastal plane, yet has a few rocky runs that look like they would fit in more with mountainous geography rather than the sandy, wooded flat it winds through.

I've always wanted to look at these stony sections of Mill Creek underwater, so I finally got up the courage to park on the shoulder of the Ikea distribution warehouse road, hop the guardrail, and weave through the thin section of woods that separate the road from the creek. This is part of Perryville Town Park, but still I feel like a trespasser.

The smell of laundry hit me as soon as I entered the woods. Perryville's treated sewage discharge is one hundred yards upstream from the boulder rich run I was about to enter, and the water smelled like it. I lay on the cobbled bottom and saw what I expected: algae covered rocks, a sign of too much nitrogen. But the algae wasn't the usual monochromatic greenish, tan-gray mat coating everything. It was stringy and dark green and waved in the strong current. I dragged myself upstream along the bottom into a deeper hole. Black-nosed dace schooled in the bottom of the one foot depression, and took turns darting through the current. The black horizontal stripes on their sides show dramatically against what looks like gold body backgrounds. They were the fish I thought were real finds when I was a kid. It was a special day when we caught a "striper" as we called them on the Pumpkin Patch Creek in Colonia. They are one of the most abundant coastal plain fish, and have the ability to survive in pretty heavily urbanized streams, so the rarity of us catching them on the Pumpkin Patch was probably more related to their speed and our limited seine net skill rather than a lack of abundance.

While they are abundant here, they aren't the only species in Mill Creek. Tessellated darters smugly held their ground on the gravely shoals behind larger rocks. Banded killifish sluggishly changed their position in the stream compared to the fast moves of the darters. Large schools of small bluegill filled deeper holes, and I'm pretty sure I saw the ghostly outline of a northern hogsucker glide along the bottom.

This creek is right on the edge of historic brook trout range. The habitat certainly could support brookies, and I can imagine multiple darter species here along with stone pile nest-building chubs. Maybe we can get Mill Creek, and other streams, back to what they were. The fish diversity that remains and a few sprigs of aquatic moss covering a few rocks offer glimmers of hope. Hope in a restored Mill Creek even with a sewage treatment plant emitting high nutrient effluent a few hundred feet upstream.

Even the ugly and perceived dead streams, like Laurel Hill, the Little North East, and this stretch of Mill Creek, have beauty. Some of that beauty is in witnessing how life finds a way. That life is here gives me hope that we can work to restore impacted streams to a less degraded state than where they are now. There is still life in significantly degraded creeks. If life can survive those conditions, imagine what can happen when we act for clean water. The things we need to do for clean water aren't complicated. They just take a little thought and intention. Think about where the water goes after it runs off your roof top or driveway. Install rain gardens to help filter it before it gets to that small stream or ditch. Keep your car tuned up and fix oil drips. Drive the most fuel efficient low emission car you can. Don't spray herbicides in ditches or on stream banks. Conserve water. Encourage local officials to use green infrastructure to control storm water runoff. These are not complicated solutions. It just take some will and life can come back to its full abundance and diversity. It has been shown time and again that when we give life half a chance it restores. And that is beautiful.

Turbidity

I used to avoid the larger eddies, those areas of sluggish water behind rocks and shoreline aberrations. The slower moving water created by the upstream obstruction allows the finest silt particles to settle to the bottom and expanses of barren mud-covered flats extend downstream. I always thought of muddy eddies as lifeless, and I usually created chocolate milk water conditions by accidentally stirring the fine bottom before I could really see who was living in these areas.

I skimmed over one of these eddies on my way to what I thought was the more interesting habitat of a cobbled riffle, when I came upon a line in the mud that led five feet or so to a Virginia river snail slowly but surely making its way upstream. In the moment I paused to admire the snail, other life became apparent. Tiny squiggles of new fish schooled in a small hazy cloud. Black smudges of other kinds of fry swam toward me to investigate. Toad poles shaped like commas squiggled along the bottom. The importance of the perceived lifeless barren became apparent: it was a nursery for the stream. Suddenly, the barren wasn't so barren.

Sedimentation results in the loss of habitat and is one of the leading causes of stream degradation. Sediment turns water cloudy, clogs fish gills, and makes feeding for some fish species very difficult. For example, rosy-sided dace don't tolerate turbidity very well, and just a small increase impacts their ability to pluck insects from the current. It's hard to catch what you can't see. As we disturb land in the watershed through construction and agriculture, more soil washes into the stream which increases the turbidity of the water and there are times when I wonder if our rivers will finally reach some threshold of turbidity as their watersheds become more suburbanized and the effort of hunting isn't worth the return for these fish so they leave.

The inputs of soil we send to our streams through ground-disturbing activities like farming and construction, and scouring runoff that comes from hard surfaces like driveways and roads needs to be controlled. But small amounts of erosion and resulting sedimentation are natural processes, and the fine muds that form the bottom of these eddies are important in the continuum of stream habitats—from quiet muddy eddies, to violent boulder-filled rapids. Life has evolved and developed to nestle in a particular spot on the spectrum, and all habitats are essential. Even the muddy ones.

Mud in moderation is good, but people often perceive that there's nothing to see in rivers and streams because of turbidity. I heard a diver describe local diving conditions as braille diving because you dive by feel; the visibility is that poor. I used the same language when I was an avid diver and knew that there wasn't much to see on the bottom of the deeper holes on the Susquehanna, or in the quarries turned diving destinations. But still, his comment bothered me, even if he did have a point. Maybe it was because that perpetuated the attitude that there isn't anything of worth or value to see or protect in the rivers and streams in our neighborhoods, which certainly isn't the case.

But I think his comment hit a nerve because I caught the same attitude creeping into my psyche. There's a seasonality to water clarity here, and it seemed that the better summer visibility was really late in arriving. It seemed that in the week prior I'd walked to the water's edge, gear bag in hand, watched clouds of sediments blur the bottom, shaken my head, turned around, and gone home more than I got into the water.

Maybe the comment from that diver bothered me because my reality, living in the developed east, is muddy water, compared to other places where streams run clear because they traverse large green expanses on the map like our National Forests.

So when I got to the Octoraro one night and saw less than clear water, my first inclination was to turn around. But it had been a few days since I'd been in any water, and it was hot, so I decided to get wet.

I crept along in a foot of water with the bottom in clear view. Three feet of visibility might mean you can't see anything in 60 feet of water, but in a foot of water everything is sharp. A small mouth bass confronted me behind his rock, circled around and confronted me again. It must have been in his territory. Further upstream, the water deepened, and things on the bottom of the four foot hole were hazy, but recognizable. I floated over a two foot long catfish. A small rapid dumps into the deeper pool, and I let the upstream eddy carry me into it.

A few male satinfin shiners were in a dog fight over prime breeding terrain. Their dainty iridescent blue dorsal fins and silver white pectoral and pelvic fins fluttered and flared like butterflies in a stiff breeze. They spun around each other in a tight circle, broke chase, and then spun again. I was able to watch this mid-water column display of glowing blue and silver-white for quite some time as the males defended their spot, and enticed females, while creek chubs fed on the bottom.

One of the males mistook me for another satinfin shiner and flared right in front of my mask. The shiner came nose to nose with me and stuck his pale blue pectoral fins out stiffly as if to communicate *this spot is mine, move on*. Maybe he saw his reflection in the lens. Either way it was an incredible display. The water was murky, and I couldn't make out more than the outline of a large bedrock slab four feet away. But that didn't matter. I had enough visibility to witness the beauty and drama of the Octoraro that evening. This trip showed me that even when conditions are less than ideal, there are still amazing things to witness, intricate processes to experience. I used to let cloudy water conditions keep me out of rivers. But I need to get in water, the way runners need to run and painters need to paint, and snorkeling, even in turbid conditions, fills that need. I don't feel right when there are long lapses between snorkeling adventures. There are days when I can't wait to get underwater, to become enveloped by the silence and the white noise rush of water over rock. To only exist in the moment. River snorkeling always brings me to the here and now.

A small but intense thunderstorm traversed the upper parts of Deer Creek's watershed, and, while the surface of the creek barely rose, the water became murky with soil in water runoff. I couldn't see much but that didn't matter. I skulked upstream, clambered over rocks, held on and dug in. I used eddies to work my way up river.

The creek slackened into a deep pool and I explored the margins. Fry squiggled through the slower moving water. An eel darted along the bottom when my shadow passed over. A bass shot from under a rock. The bright day made seeing what lay in the shadow of rock impossible until my head was well shrouded in the dark, which was a little disconcerting. The unknown, even in a known river, is unsettling, and I fully expected to see a foot long hellbender lunge out from the dusk.

While there wasn't much to clearly see in the way of fish, the up close macro world was plainly in view, and just as fascinating. Snails rasped trails through the algae that covered rocks. Hydropsche caddis nets captured more than their share of fine sediments. The world around me was silent, except for the gurgle of water flowing past my ears, and the occasional clicking that I suspect is produced by stonerollers as they snap algae off boulders. I watched the water sheet over rocks, and the problems of the day washed away with each eddy that swirled past. There is something rejuvenating about being encapsulated in water, even when it's cloudy. One of the constant struggles of creek snorkeling is finding clear water between rain events.

I expected Mill Creek to be pristine, but some streams that look unspoiled aren't, depending on how we use their watersheds. Mill Creek flows through a deep hemlock and rhododendron forested gorge over shelves of moss and fern covered Wissahickon schist, the metallic slate blue bedrock that folds in ropy bands and forms the hilly terrain of the lower Susquehanna Valley. I know this creek from the surface and have been hiking through its minor chasm for 20 years.

It was hot and humid at the top of the steep bank above Mill Creek that day, but the summertime stickiness was soon replaced with refreshing cool as I descended over smooth slabs of bedrock, cooled no doubt by the cold water cascading over multiple stair step falls. This, I thought, was a trout quality stream, and I envisioned trophy fish hovering in the eddy formed on the sides of the last chute that enters this pool.

I slipped into the water and was instantly enveloped in a cloud of silt. A few inches of fine ooze coated everything. If there were trout here, I couldn't see them through the thick haze, but I doubted they could survive the silt. There was no habitat variability in the deep pool, no rocky bottom, just a layer of mud. My perception of the creek, based on its outward appearance, was all wrong, and a look at the larger watershed beyond the narrow sliver of hemlock canyon revealed that the only reason the Mill Creek ravine had old hemlock and rhododendron covering its sides is because it was too steep to farm. Any land that was farmable in the area, was, and disturbed land like farm fields results in erosion. Eroded soils flow into streams, cloud water, and settle to the bottom where they smother benthic life. Stream bottoms normally have an abundance of nooks and crannies formed by different sized rocks stacked on one another. They normally have a diversity of habitats. Streams that are sedimented in, like this one, have a homogenous mud flat bottom, and no trout.

Mill Creek's eastern sister is Tucquan Creek. While Mill Creek cascades through Wissahickon schist bedrock on the western shore of the Susquehanna, Tucquan Creek does the same on the eastern shore. On the surface both look similar: their paths are carved through hemlock and rhododendron gorges. I didn't expect much as I masked up. I figured I would see the same murk I had in Mill Creek. But Tucquon turned out to be different. Everything was covered by mud there too, but not as much, and the water was less hazy. I could see a foot or two. And there was life. A crayfish ambled past me, as tiny fry wriggled upstream in the soft shoreline current. Black-nosed and rosy-sided dace darted through the strong center flow, and a few trout eluded my camera as they scattered on the bottom of a deeper pool.

An aerial view reveals the source of the difference in these creek sisters: Trees. The Tucquan Creeks watershed contains much more forest than Mill Creek's, and the result is less sediment, clearer water, and more life. How we use land miles from the nearest stream affects that stream and the potential for life to exist in it. Watershed beyond the stream corridor matters.

I plan group snorkeling trips around where I think the clear water will be. Sometimes it feels like we have years of muddy summer time water. A line of typical summer afternoon thunderstorms moved through our region the day before a trip I had planned for a group of college aged National Aquarium interns. A lot of the rain hit land that was disturbed by farming or construction activities which resulted in soil clouding the runoff, and our streams. A lot of the water ran from hard surfaces like roads, driveways, and rooftops which scoured more soil into our streams. The result was really murky water in the stream where I'd planned to take this group snorkeling. I decided we would try the Susquehanna first. The river usually experiences very slow flows in the summer, and the water gets very clear.

We slipped into the river below Conowingo Dam and watched a herd of Virginia river sails graze algae off rocks, watched a few sunnies defend their nests, and saw the shadows of a few smallmouth bass stay just barely in view. Conowingo Dam is a hydro electric power plant and it releases water though its turbines to generate electricity. Conowingo started to let the river flow through its turbines to generate power. The warning lights placed on some of the islands and along the shoreline went off to tell everyone the river was going to rise and the current was going to get fast, and they did. The increased flow kicked sediment into the water, which reduced visibility, so we left.

I still had a half a day of snorkeling to fill and was out of options, I thought. We went to Deer Creek, our usual go to, and as assumed earlier in the morning, it was brown with sediment. As the group ate lunch I scoped out a smaller tributary to the Susquehanna. It's a rocky, boulder strewn creek, barely ten feet wide, that tumbles down the hills of the lower Susquehanna Valley. It's not very deep, maybe a foot in a few holes, but the water runs clear.

We explored this small tributary after lunch, and watched an entirely different aquatic community of black-nosed dace, common shiner, and crayfish in a choreographed ecological ballet, each species attending to its appointed niche and place in the stream. The dace plucked at the sandy bottom of the slower parts, the shiners fed in our wakes, where all the insects we inadvertently kicked off the bottom flowed, and the crayfish scavenged.

As the year ended I found myself experience the same problem. Every time my schedule opened up to allow a snorkeling trip, it rained, our rivers got muddy, and I got frustrated. Then I checked some of the smaller steams, and found that they ran clear.

I got into the water of Elbow Branch, a tiny sliver of a creek, barely deep enough for me to float. I experienced the familiar but always awe inspiring force water exerts even in small streams, and was transported into another realm. As I hovered in the creek, a darter shot from beneath me and let the current wrap its body around another rock. Caddisfly larvae grazed. I floated and watched until I started to shiver in the barely above freezing conditions. This confirmed it. The water isn't as big, and the larger fish and fish schools aren't here, but there's amazing life to see in the smaller tributaries.

It's easy for me to get pessimistic about the future of our aquatic environments when water clarity depends on mini droughts. But finding clear water to snorkel gives hope. I've learned that I can always find water clear enough in which to snorkel. One of those streams is Stony Run. I've driven over the little non-descript and forgotten stream hundreds of times on my way to and from work, and each time I peer over the low barricade on the short bridge to get a glimpse of the water.

Every time it looks clear, even after heavy rains. But it's a small creek and not very accessible due to fast traffic and overgrown banks so I've never considered exploring it.

I decided to snorkel the stream when I became frustrated with the seemingly perpetual murky condition of other streams in the area due to flashy downpours earlier in the summer season. Stony Run never seemed to be affected, and I wondered if that was just an illusion, or if the water really was clearer. I struggled through the climbing bittersweet and poison ivy, to get to a pool that was out of sight from the road. I was paranoid about being confused with a body.

As soon as I stuck my face in it, I knew the water was clearer. Fish were abundant and diverse. Tessellated and Johnny darters sent small puffs of sediment into the water with every jerky leap off the bottom. Chubs slowly came in to explore what I was, and nervously shot off into the distance. A common shiner in its reddish breeding color danced before me as blue gill and pumpkin seeds put on aggressive displays to defend their nests. A small school of northern hog sucker worked the bottom and I'm pretty sure I saw a stoneroller. It was like swimming in an aquarium. While the water is clear, it isn't without issues. Algae covers everything.

I checked out this tiny gem on the map, to try to determine why it stays clear when many of the other streams in the area turn brown after rains. Stony Run's watershed is about 40% developed, mostly in new houses. So, it should be as muddy as the others, unless the storm water management requirements of newer construction, like storm water retention ponds, work. Maybe that's why Stony Run is clear, but over-fertilized. We've required storm water reducing technology to reduce heavy flows that come from impervious surfaces. Technology like storm water retention ponds which mimic the function of natural storm water reducing systems like wetlands and forests, and allow heavy flows to soak into the ground back into ground water, rather than runoff hard and fast. This reduces scouring runoff from reaching streams, which results in clearer water. But we haven't done too much yet to control nitrogen runoff, which makes the stringy algae that covers everything in the stream.

Stony Run gives me hope that maybe newer storm water management regulations do work in reducing sediment loads to our streams, which translates to healthier streams and clearer water to snorkel. And lots of fish to see.

Floods

I dropped into the clear water and didn't expect to experience the force I did in the foot deep current. Basin Run is a smaller creek that cascades down boulder terraces to flow through sandy and rock bottomed pools. Most of its watershed is still forested so the water there is clearer than in most other creeks on the Mid-Atlantic slope, though technically Basin Run is right on the cusp of coastal plain and piedmont, in that brief transition between the two major geographies.

I inched myself upstream by digging my toes and fingers into the gravel covered benthos. Eddies behind larger rocks caused sand tornadoes to swirl up from the bottom into the water. The creek was still rearranging after the last large rain event remodeled the pool. Three weeks prior, the clear, foot deep section had been five feet deeper and chocolate milk brown after a heavy rain had fallen on the region in the span of a day. The two foot diameter tree trunks stacked like tooth picks against a car-sized boulder were a testament to, and reminder of, the force and fury this place had endured.

These torrents seem to be occurring more frequently, and one of the predicted consequences of global warming is a flashier rain pattern for the eastern United States. Rain events may become less frequent and more intense, and flows in our creeks reflect the weather pattern. There's a good chance the flows in our streams will dwindle between rain storms, then overflow banks, flood, and rearrange creek beds when it does rain. Feast and famine hydrology.

We can't say much about climate after only a few seasons, but it seems that the summer weather norm on the East Coast is becoming monsoonal. Lots of rain with lots of muddy runoff. Maybe Bill McKibben in his book *The End of Nature* was right. Maybe we ended nature. Maybe the climate is now dictated by us and so too is the new flash hydrology of streams.

Another potential effect of climate change is that the dates of first ice on our rivers comes later, and last ice leaves earlier. I wonder if ice will become a thing of the past, a legend, and if I will tell stories of how our creeks used to freeze, and how we played hockey on the neighborhood stream to my grandkids the way my grandfather used to tell stories of how the Raritan used to ice over so thick you could drive across it, from Perth Amboy New Jersey to Staten Island.

The fact that the climate is changing doesn't scare me. That's what climates do. Where do you think all the coal in Pennsylvania came from? From when Pennsylvania was a humid swamp three hundred million years ago during a period that lasted for 34 million years, when its climate was much more tropical. What I fear is the rate of this change. I can see changes in my lifetime, changes that should take much, much, longer. It's hard to deny that we have sped up the process with our fossil fuel addiction.

I fear changes to our climate mostly for selfish reasons. I don't want to see our streams change before I know them. After years of snorkeling the same creeks I feel like I am just now beginning to understand them, how life adjusts to season, how fish respond to rains and droughts, how the creek changes with flow. There are so many streams to snorkel at different times of day in different seasons; I can never see them all. Forget about even trying to understand them all. And now that I have just barely scratched the surface of really understanding the ecology of a handful of creeks, it stands to change dramatically.

Cold water fisheries may be no more; community composition will change. The breeding ecology of a lot of species is based on water temperatures. Exotic species whose spread is partly controlled by colder temperatures are primed to expand their range with mellow winters. Hydrology will probably be altered, maybe to flood and drought without much in between. This isn't all doom and gloom; life will find a way. But it will probably be different, and possibly before I have had the chance to watch and learn the current system.

Basin Run is a small creek just a few minutes from my house and is always good for a variety of fish. I watched a mixed school of black-nosed dace, rosy-sided dace, and common shiner dance amid the air bubbles where the water drops over a boulder shelf into their pool, to learn how they live. They lunged with wide open mouths and I assumed they were plucking food items I couldn't see from the water. The fish grew used to my presence and I felt like I was weaving and bobbing with them as part of the school. The rosy-sided dace looked like miniature salmon with their red sides and strong swimming strokes and all of them seem to look brighter against the bottom; all of the sediments had been washed from the gravel and sand so that the orange and milk white colors of the quartz pebbles showed.

How had those fish survived the last big flow that resulted from the last big rain? How had the fish been able to stay in the creek through the last torrent? Where had they ridden out the storm? One way to find out: gear up and get wet during the next big downpour. Maybe those observations would partially inform the question: what affect would the potential, predicted global warming-induced changes to the hydrology of our creeks have on the fish?

There is great adventure that comes from snorkeling during floods, that is spawned from the very real danger of drowning. It's not the smartest activity, but it is exhilarating, and I approached Basin Run to answer some of these questions after a hard rain. It had stopped raining about an hour prior but still I was nervous. There is a lag time between when rain hits the ground and when creek levels rise and there had been quite a bit of rain in a short amount of time, at least an inch in an hour. There was a good possibility that Basin Run would rise even more.

However, Basin Run's watershed was still dominated by forest, which would work in my favor just like it works in the favor of the fish and insects that live in the creek. Forests act as huge sponges and absorb incredible quantities of rain. Rather than all of that water making a hard and fast beeline for the nearest stream, and scouring the stream bed when it arrives, rain in a forested watershed soaks into the ground, and is filtered as it slowly travels to the nearest stream. The creek still rises, but much more gradually than streams in a watershed whose forest has been removed—or worse— replaced with surfaces that don't allow rain to soak in like roof tops and roads. When rain hits these hard surfaces, it runs off directly into the local stream without being filtered. These unfiltered rains contaminate the stream with pollutants like nitrogen and mercury it picks up from the atmosphere and gas, oil, and antifreeze the rain picks up as it runs over hard surfaces. Streams with forested buffers don't flood as frequently as creeks with suburbanized watersheds. Suburbanized streams tend to flash flood regularly, their water levels rapidly rise and drop off just as fast. Somehow, organisms in these streams are able to hang on.

I couldn't see the stream through the woods, but I could hear its rush. Branches of trees that had fallen into the stream strained out whatever was in the current that was large enough to get trapped in the tangle. Strong currents in streams and rivers trap things against strainers and hold them underwater. Water is deceptively strong, and escape from strainers is nearly impossible. They are very dangerous features to anyone in moving water.

A fallen tree spanned the width of the creek just downstream of the pool I snorkeled, and strained the entire flow of Basin Run. On a normal day it's not a threat. When the creek is high, ending up in that strainer would be lethal, and based on the volume of sound that came from the creek, it could be one of those lethal days if the current were to peel my grip from the bottom.

I knelt in the water at the edge of the bank and the strong current piled water up to my chin. It was hard to hold position even kneeling and I wasn't sure if going in was a good idea. I got a solid grasp of large boulders on the bottom and submerged. The world was chaos. Particles flew by too fast to identify. The creek was loud, even underwater. I could only move upstream at a crawling pace. I made sure I had three solid points of contact with the bottom before I made any move, the way a rock climber assures the same. I was very aware that I would only have 50 yards to stop myself before hitting the strainer, and in this flow that would be difficult. I didn't see any fish.

I lateraled out to the center of the stream. Fifty pound boulders peeled off the bottom as I tried to not get swept away. I didn't see any fish after each rock moved from the bottom. It didn't appear they were hunkered down in the substrate. I started to pick larger rocks to hang on to. The water grabbed at my mask and tried to pull it from my face. My snorkel hummed. I moved into a chute and the force of the water plucked me from the bottom and sent me tumbling through the rapid. I clawed at the bottom to stop but every rock I grabbed just peeled away. I didn't have time to become afraid. I had to arrest my descent or I would get caught in the strainer, and drown. Then I would join the ranks of stupid people who drowned. "What the hell was he doing in the creek on a day like today anyway?" I didn't want the post mortem embarrassment. My hands clawed at the bottom. I dropped my feet, hoping my toes would hit a rock and stop my downstream trajectory without my legs getting trapped in a void. It worked and I made my way to a large eddy behind a boulder embedded in the shore. My heart caught up with the realization of how dangerous that was, how close I came to drowning, and beat loudly in my ears. Adrenaline filled my blood and a huge grin emerged across my face. This was living. It was being in the moment when nothing else but survival mattered. It was living life on the rivers terms. A trout darted out as I floated in, which answered part of my earlier question. At least the trout rode out heavy flows in the eddy.

Gravel bars formed in long *V*s behind rocks in the stream. Sand bars were created, dissolved, and reformed. Small cobbles bounced down the bottom. Some aspects of creeks are very ephemeral, like sand bars, a temporary place in between structures of some permanence like boulders and bedrock. But water wears and shapes even these, just as water shapes our lives, our communities, our societies and cultures. Our effect on the global climate affects it all. It is all connected—rock, water, weather, fish, and human, and questions of their current and future interactions remain.

Nuclear Shadow

Three Mile Island scared the crap out of me when I was 12. It came close to melting down and I remember being very concerned for my aunt, who lived in a nearby town that would have been eliminated had the ultimate disaster happened. I went to see the movie *The China Syndrome* not long after and that cemented my hate for nuclear power that lasted through young adulthood. I have mellowed a bit with age, and now recognize that the culprits in all energy related calamities are us. We are the ones that create the demand, and demand cheap energy. Not that the oil, coal, or nuclear power companies are free from sin, but I've learned that when I'm wagging my finger at someone else, three are pointing back at me.

I slid into the water upstream of the Three Mile Island nuclear power plant at the canal lock recreation area. I wanted to see what lived there, but mostly to dispel the growing perception that there's no life worth watching in the Susquehanna, and the act of getting into it will make you sick. The Lock Haven Dam is just downstream from that, and backs up the Susquehanna to supply cooling water to Three Mile Island, and potential energy to the York Haven Dam and Powerhouse. Just about anywhere I've snorkeled on the Susquehanna is affected by energy production in some way, and the water from the lower river is used by hydro, nuclear, and coal fired plants to give us the energy we need to maintain our lifestyles.

The river at that point is typical Susquehanna—big, expansive, shallow water, with numerous rock outcrops. An assortment of invasive shells—an invasive jambalaya of sorts: mystery snails, corbicula, and rusty crayfish carapaces, were piled in a dry eddy.

Five crayfish rocketed in different directions. They were everywhere, and I couldn't make any move without causing one to shoot off out of sight. They were the invasive rusty crayfish, with large claws and rust colored patches on the sides of their carapaces. They were so abundant, they must surely have an effect on the ecology there, especially on the benthos. Rusty-sided crayfish reduce numbers of bottom dwelling insects and other invertebrates, and displace some fish species, especially bluegill, smallmouth and largemouth bass, and walleye. They deprive native fish of their prey and cover and out-compete native crayfish.

There were lots of dead shells of another invasive, the Chinese mystery snail, but where were the live animals? Wedged down in the substrate? Invasives, like many of the crayfish, Chinese mystery snails—and now for the Susquehanna, zebra mussels—are one of the leading causes of globally declining freshwater biodiversity.

Benthic fish, like tessellated darters, didn't seem to be affected, since they appeared to be as abundant as other places I've snorkeled without such high numbers of these fish. Virginia river snails were also common and they left grazed patches and trails where they'd eaten the slick biofilm on the smooth slabs of bedrock, but they might be affected. They looked less abundant than in other places below Conowingo Dam, near the mouth of the Susquehanna. Maybe Virginia river snails were less abundant than other places because of the crayfish. Were the crayfish affecting the darters or smallmouth bass, whose numbers in the Susquehanna had recently dropped? Were they affecting the snails or other invertebrates?

It was all conjecture and hard to say. It's certain that Three Mile Island was a very different place than when the first Europeans arrived. The system I observed in a few feet of water little resembled the ecosystem pre-European settlement. We have rearranged the place hydrologically, geologically, and biologically. We removed coal from the ground and sent it down the river to market. Coal dust from shipments gone wrong still fills cracks in the exposed bedrock. We built numerous walls to hold water back, to create lakes to supply water for power plants and we built other walls to keep water out of our cities and towns. We engineered structures to meet our needs, rather than the needs of the river. We added creatures like the crayfish and mystery snails that completely changed the biological complexion of the river. And the hydrology is different. We pull more water from the river each year and competing priorities—municipal water for towns, irrigation for farms, cooling water for power plants, minimum flows for hydropower—require the formation of commissions to decide water allocations.

I explored all of the intricate submerged folds in the bedrock that form a maze of passages. Small mouth bass played hide and seek, and I chased a few fish that I swear were log perch, but didn't get a good enough look for a positive identification. Water willow, a stiff plant with stout green leaves, bamboo like shoots, and small white and purple flowers that resemble orchids, covered the small sand bars that form in the exposed lee and crannies of the bedrock islands. Turtles sunned themselves on some of the bedrock outcrops and plopped into the river when I approached. I lost track of where I was in the river so I peeked above the water line to get my bearings. There before me, in the background of a water willow island, were the towers of Three Mile Island.

This is used water. Power companies pull it from the river to cool their nuclear power plants. Industry uses it to make the things we deem as necessary for our way of life. Cities pump water from the river to our houses so we can drink it, bathe in it, and flush our excrement away in it. Bass fishermen launch at the nearby ramp to use the river for recreation and I use it to explore, to experience discovery and adventure. But this isn't unique to the Susquehanna. Any river in North America is heavily used. And I wonder what the biggest danger is, or will all these threats work in synergy to finally destroy whatever is left of our freshwater ecosystems? While this is far from pre-European pristine, there is still a lot left to protect.

Fish Declines

The bottom of the pools looked gray from the bridge. But the gray patches moved. I knew the pools we full of shad. I walked fast, like a kid on a pool deck, down off the bridge, down the embankment to the shore of Deer Creek. I suited up quickly. So fast that I almost forgot to zip my dry suit closed. I waded into the river, and when I got close to the first pool, lay down in the two foot deep water.

Before I thought I should, I was surrounded by foot long fish, all moving in unison. I found a large rock, planted my feet on the upstream side and stretched out into the current. The shad were jittery and each time I cleared water from my snorkel, each time a car drove over the bridge above me, or each time I got too sideways to the current and was thrown off the rock that kept me propped against that current, they scattered with panicked jerky movements. But soon they returned to their upstream quest and rhythmic, almost mesmerizing, undulations.

The school, a few hundred fish strong, was made up of gizzard shad and smaller river herring, and it looked like each pool held about the same number. They all swam together and presented their sides to me to form a wall of fish. Swimming with this many fish is always a thrill. But the fact that many of the fish in the school were endangered American shad made the experience that much more special. To think that I was surrounded by possibly hundreds of a kind of animal that is at risk of dying off gave me hope that the fish would make it. I also felt honored to be witness to their incredible run, to possibly be one of the last humans to see such a sight. I have hope for the shad, but it is a guarded optimism.

Shad used to be incredibly abundant and perhaps stories of them swimming so thick you could walk across rivers on their backs without getting your feet wet had some credibility. Each spring in the 1800s, a net was strung across the mouth of the Susquehanna, between Perryville and Havre de Grace, and the entire local economy was seasonally driven by the shad run. Shad are migratory fish and spend most of their lives at sea. They migrate into freshwater to spawn. Their decline started when we started to dam rivers. Shad couldn't get past the obstructions to get to their spawning grounds, so reproduction declined. Couple decreased reproduction with increased sediment loads due to deforestation and heavy fishing pressure, and their numbers dropped.

The negative effect dams had on migratory shad was recognized early. The state of Pennsylvania has required fish passages on dams since the 1800s. Unfortunately, the passages installed were poorly designed and did little to restore fish migration routes. Even today, many passages are only marginally effective. We are good at destroying, not so good at restoring.

Conowingo Dam has two fish lifts installed, essentially a kind of elevator that carries fish one hundred feet up where they swim under Route 1 into the water behind the dam. It seemed the multi-million dollar investment reversed the trend of declining American Shad populations at Conowingo Dam a few years ago, and then another unexplained decline occurred in a population that is already at historic lows.

Turns out that the latest threat to the shad may be rockfish. Rockfish eat menhaden. Menhaden are forage fish in the same family as shad. We are learning that rockfish switch to eating shad when menhaden numbers are down. The menhaden fishery has been largely unregulated, and as many fish as possible are sucked from the Bay and converted to cosmetics and fertilizers. At the same time, rockfish made a tremendous comeback after a moratorium on their take. Of course this isn't the definite cause of the more recent shad decline, but to me it seems the most plausible. Either that or all the engineering the power companies have invested in, all the fish lifts constructed to get shad above the dams, have been folly, the idea that we can engineer ourselves out of any problem flawed.

As John Muir said, when we look at any one thing in the universe, we find it hitched to everything else, and that certainly applies to the fish world. Our actions matter. As I swam with this wall of fish, I certainly felt that connection.

Abundance doesn't mean safe from decline. The passenger pigeon should have taught us that. The shad story reinforces it, and the Susquehanna River smallmouth bass fishery provides another example.

The Susquehanna supported a world class smallmouth bass fishery that attracted people from all over the world. In 2005, fishermen began reporting thousands of dead and dying young bass, and that trend hasn't changed. Today, what was once a world class fishery is at risk of total collapse. All in the span of only 15 years. A single cause hasn't been identified, but some possible culprits include fertilizers and pesticides used in farming, endocrine disrupting pharmaceuticals like estrogen in birth control, invasive green algae blooms that are caused by high phosphorous loads, and flame retardants that wash from clothes. All of these don't come from the end of a single pipe, but rather are non-point pollutants. They come from multiple places, from all of us, and are much more difficult to control than point source pollutants that can be regulated at a single point of entry into our waters.

The smallmouth bass mating ritual I watched in five feet of water on the lower Susquehanna had much more significance due to their current precarious state. The female stayed stationary on the bottom. The smaller male circled tightly around her and came alongside her. Their tails beat vigorously together for a minute then they both rocketed off. They came back to the same spot and repeated the process.

I hoped I wasn't watching the last of smallmouth reproducing on the Susquehanna. I hope the young these bass produce survive. I hope we figure out the cause of the smallmouth decline, and that we have the fortitude required to take the necessary steps to protect water quality and reverse the decline. I hope the Susquehanna once again becomes a world class fishery, and I hope my grandkids can watch shad runs and smallmouth courtship when they snorkel the Susquehanna.

Rock Snot

The Gunpowder River still looks and feels almost pristine, even though it flows through some of the most developed real estate in the east. Its steep valley is largely protected in a state park. It's a river in my region, like many, that I have explored little from beneath the surface. It's a river I want to spend more time with, to learn it.

I pulled into the parking lot of the old Monkton Train station in north eastern Maryland on the North Central Rail Trail, and saw a wader wash. Not a good sign. I knew didymo was in the Gunpowder, but I didn't know it was in this section. Wader wash stations had been installed to keep fishermen from spreading the algae.

Didymo is a diatomaceous alga that is originally from northern Europe and Asia; it has spread worldwide. It coats everything in the stream with a thick, dark olive brown mucous-like material. Hence its common name: rock snot. Since it smothers the stream bottom, it kills aquatic insects and robs the stream of diverse habitat, which translates into less fish diversity.

The ironic thing about didymo is that the people degrading streams by spreading the algae are the same ones who probably love creeks the most. Pieces of didymo can become attached to waders (or snorkeling gear). When the fisherman steps into a different stream the didymo washes off and can infect the new stream. Hence the wader wash. Even I can bring it with me on my snorkeling gear.

I had another trip planned that day to check on the progress of the spring herring run in another stream. The herring trip was more critical than the Gunpowder exploration since the herring are only in our streams for a short while and I could explore the Gunpowder any time. I normally decontaminate my gear by thoroughly drying it between trips. I wouldn't have been able to do that between the two swims I had planned so I chose to not get into the Gunpowder. I didn't want to risk spreading didymo.

A few weeks later I snorkeled Deer Creek. I am always on the lookout for new discoveries when I snorkel. Departments of Natural Resources just don't have enough funding to put a lot of people out monitoring, so I often act as an extra set of eyes when I'm in creeks. Deer Creek is supposed to be didymo free, but I found a clump of wiry, snot-like algae on a rock. I contacted a friend of mine who is a fisheries biologist.

"Matt, I think I found some didymo in Deer Creek."

"Shit. I hope not," Pete crackled over a poor cell phone connection. "Bag it up and take it to the Annapolis office. We will have someone look at it."

I scooped up the algae and dropped it at the lab as instructed. A few days later I got an email that said what I'd found wasn't didymo. It was some form of filamentous algae. We all breathed a collective sigh of relief. Our streams are under enough pressure, they don't need the added stress of an invasive alga.

However, our understanding of Didymo is changing. The newest science reported by *Scientific American* in 2014 indicates that didymo may be native to North America, based on DNA analysis, but the environmental conditions needed to trigger its visible growth were previously absent. The reasons we are seeing blooms of the alga may be related to climate change and low phosphorous loads. While most algal blooms are caused by an excess of phosphorous, didymo blooms are caused by too little phosphorous. Human-induced environmental changes could be causing didymo blooms in pristine rivers around the world, and in the Gunpowder.

Native or not, when conditions are right, didymo becomes invasive and causes a shift in the invertebrate population from large bodied species to smaller species, which can negatively affect the fish community. And the right conditions for this explosive growth, we are learning, are influenced by us.

Dams

As I watched the Susquehanna River, the Conowingo dam opened a few turbines to meet Philadelphia's demand for electricity. Conowingo is in Maryland, ten miles from the mouth of the Susquehanna, but the electricity it generates is supplied to Philadelphia rather than the local community. I really don't understand electricity distribution. The dam operator had predicted that the volume of river flowing through would go from 5,000 cubic feet per second to 32,000 cubic feet per second an hour later. This is a relatively gentle flow. Most days the river goes from 5,000 cubic feet per second to 70,000 cubic feet per second. But still, I debated whether it would be safe to enter the water as I watched how the flow changed from the shore while the river perceptibly rose. I cautiously tested the force of the current, realized that I could hold my place in the river, and started to snorkel.

The water was a blizzard of flocculent sediments that washed from the bottom and streamed by like sideways blowing snow. Normally erect water willow were matted to the bottom by the current. Virginia river snails sheltered at the bases of cobbles large enough not to move in the flow. Expanses of water willow that covered low gravel islands when the dam wasn't generating power were now underwater and provided new places for small fish to feed and hide. The rising water exposed more habitat, and tessellated darters, minnows, and the fry of unknown species all used the emerging forest.

As harsh as the rapidly changing environment appeared to be, it seemed that organisms living there had adapted to the artificial tide established by the dam. Just like organisms living in a tidal system, some headed for the cover of water willow and cobble on the bottom when flow increased and the water rose. Others foraged on the newly flooded habitat, some emerged again when the flow subsided. The only difference was that the Conowingo tide is controlled by electrical demand rather than gravitational pull.

Dams alter downstream flow regimes, and they also completely change upstream ecosystems. For example, Jordan Creek is a heavily controlled creek in Allentown, PA corralled by stone masonry walls that have been placed to keep the river channel static. Exactly what streams don't do: stay still. Stream channels meander across valleys over time. They shift and move and shift again, and the walls that keep Jordan Creek static were the first sign it was a highly altered, artificial river system. The walls sever the natural link between the stream and its floodplain.

Trout were abundant, probably because they were recently stocked as part of a "put and take" fishery. Fisheries managers put hatchery raised rainbow trout in streams and fishermen take them out, which is just as well since the trout probably wouldn't survive on their own. Regardless, they are a west coast fish, not native to the east. In fact a few studies show that when rainbows are released into a stream their introduction significantly changes the feeding ecology of the stream since rainbow trout out-compete native fish.

But that didn't matter because I loved watching the rainbows, native or not. Besides, they were feeding with small mouth bass, another non-native top predator. Smallies are native to North America, but not this part of the continent. They are from the Mississippi River drainage and have been introduced to other areas including the Susquehanna and Delaware drainages. They have had significant negative effects on native fish by competing with and eating them. And like the rainbows they are cool to watch native or not.

Trout have sleek muscular bodies that are perfect for holding still in the strong currents found in cooler stream environments. Bass are stockier and are better at hunting in slower moving, warmer waters. While they are both top predators, they hunt in different waters so they usually don't directly compete. I'd never seen them hunting together and it was a thrill to watch them hunting side by side. Bass stayed more in the calm eddies, held their positions with minor adjustments of their pectoral fins, and waited for food to come to them when they ambushed it. Trout stayed more in the current and their tails constantly beat the water to hold their spots in the stream. They spied food morsels in the water column and lashed out to snag them.

The river was forced into a thin sheet of water over a low head dam that looked like it at one time had also served as a wet crossing for vehicles since it was about six feet wide. A red-eared slider turtle lay on the bottom of the quiet part of the plunge pool below the dam and craned its neck toward the surface to watch me watch it. Red-eareds are native to the Midwest and are common pet store turtles. This reptile could have been a pet that had gained its freedom when its keeper got tired of caring for it. Or it could have been part of the population introduced to eastern Pennsylvania that is now reproducing.

The creek above the dam was a different world, more lake than river, where thick beds of Hydrilla and Eurasian water milfoil covered the monotonous bottom. Hydrilla have hooked whorls of leaves and Eurasian water milfoil leaves are frilly tufts. Both plants are aquarium escapees and form impenetrable thickets fish can't enter. Smallmouth bass stayed just barely in view, and a stocked trout rocketed into the muddy distance. Pumpkin seed sunnies guarded their nests.

Low head dams completely change the ecology of a river. Sediments build up behind the dam and smother diverse habitat creating a monotonous sand and mud flat plane. The still water warms and becomes oxygen poor and the artificially ponded water provides habitat for artificially introduced species. Things that really don't belong in our creeks, but are at home in a pond.

Because of this, the Wildlands Conservancy and their partners have undertaken an ambitious project that will remove nine dams on the Little Lehigh and Jordan Creeks in the next few years. This will be a monumental step in restoring these streams to their natural free flowing condition, and I wanted to watch the process. Underwater.

As part of this effort I snorkeled the Little Lehigh. I entered the river a hundred yards downstream of the fish hatchery dam and crept into the current. Low head dams scare me. Even small ones. Uncertain scour holes and unpredictable currents can make even the most benign looking low head dangerous. So I approached the fish hatchery dam on the Little Lehigh with a lot of caution. The bottom is angular cobbles, all covered in an algal carpet. The stream receives excess nutrients, which makes excess algae grow, and it covers everything. That didn't seem to bother the trout that gathered in a deeper eddy in the lee of a large rock. Or the darters that flitted from the shallows into deeper water as I approached. Eutrophication, or the over-fertilization of our rivers and streams, is a problem. But maybe habitat diversity is more important.

I continued upstream and slowly entered the plunge pool of the dam. This dam wasn't more than two feet tall, but I could feel the recirculating current pull me in. I dropped my feet to the bottom and hooked my toes on some rocks. There wasn't any obvious life here. It was a violent place—loud and full of entrained air bubbles—and the bottom dropped out of view. There weren't any large fish like I'd envisioned, at least none that I could see.

Dams affect downstream as much as they do upstream. Hydraulics and hydrology, nutrient cycling and sediment flows are all affected by dams. I'm pretty sure the lack of abundant life in Little Lehigh is related to the dam. Every dam site I've snorkeled except one had less than expected numbers of fish and diversity. I was confident that pattern continued in that water as I climbed over the concrete abutment on the left side of the river and slid into the large upstream flat water expanse.

The downstream habitat was algae covered cobble—a diverse assemblage of various sizes of rocks with deeper areas where water scoured around some of the large rocks, and a shallower area where sands were deposited. This creates opportunities for a diversity of species to set up shop and live. Diverse habitat usually means diverse biology. The upstream habitat in contrast was a monotonous sand and mud flat plane. No diversity of contour, and the biology reflected it. The dam had effectively formed a desert devoid of any larger life. If there aren't places for fish to safely hunt and hide, there won't be any fish.

As I turned to float downstream I saw an Asian clam with its foot extended, feeding. The only life in the large pool that I'd witnessed that day. I stopped a few feet upstream of the dam and got out of the river. The dam was nothing more than a two-foot tall hunk of concrete, and it had outlived its usefulness, and significantly altered the ecology of the river. It's time for the dam, and the desert it formed, to go.

Fortunately, some dams never happen. The Delaware River at the Delaware Water Gap almost wasn't as it exists today. It was nearly destroyed by the placement of a dam in the 1960's. Construction on the Tocks Island Dam was supposed to start in 1967 but was stopped by a group of people who knew the destruction this dam would cause. I was grateful to have the opportunity to take a group of students snorkeling on the Delaware where the Tocks Island Dam was supposed to go 38 years prior. That might not have been possible if it hadn't been for the actions of a few committed citizens. What we do matters.

It was the second day on the Delaware River for about one hundred United Nations school students who were participating in a three day canoe trip down the Delaware with the Riverkeeper. Six of them joined me in the river to experience the underwater side of the Delaware.

Clouds of juvenile fish huddled in the lee of every large rock. The students picked out numerous juvenile freshwater mussels. Juvenile anything is good news. It means the parts of the river system are reproducing. It means the continuance of species and the critical roles they perform. In the case of mussels, it's water filtration. The Delaware River population removes sediments and algae from the water column in addition to disease causing organisms, filtering an estimated couple billion gallons of water each day.

We admired caddis fly larvae, three species of snails, and the clean river scape as we crawled our way upstream. We turned and drifted over beds of diverse submerged vegetation interspersed among clean cobble. This movement through the water is as close to flying as I have ever been able to get without being in the air, and I think the students felt the same sense of awe and freedom. None of them would have been able to experience it had Tocks Island Dam been constructed.

A few fly fishermen were wetting their lines just downstream as I stowed gear. One landed a nice buck shad. Stoneflies flew from the shoreline out over the river and I realized I was in the middle of a huge hatch. Stoneflies are indicators of good water quality. Stoney nymphs crawl from the water onto land where they metamorphose and emerge as winged adults. I watched hundreds of adults launch from the long shoreline grass.

Everything I saw in the Delaware that day was native to that stretch of river. It belonged there. Whereas everything I'd seen in Jordan Creek was artificial: non-native biology placed in an artificially constructed hydrology at the expense of a native stream scape. That doesn't mean the Jordan Creek trip hadn't been a phenomenal snorkel. Getting to see trout and bass feed side by side, and watching a red-eared slider as intrigued by me as I was by it, was absolutely incredible, and I list that urban stream experience right up there with some of the most pristine streams I've snorkeled. But it still doesn't compare to the primeval ecology of the Delaware.

"This river has a lot going for it," one of the fishermen said as he released another shad.

Yes it does. The future of the river is in our hands now, just as it was in the hands of those who decided to shelve the Tocks Island Dam idea in 1975. The decisions we make and the actions we take will dictate whether there will be juvenile fish, mussels, and students here in another 38 years. I hope we choose wisely.

Trash

It's hard for me to picture what the lower Susquehanna looked like on this day 41 years ago. Hurricane Agnes came up the Chesapeake and slowly passed over the Susquehanna. Six hundred fifty million gallons of water, mud, and silt screamed over Conowingo Dam with all 53 flood gates open as a result. This trip was the exact opposite. I tried to picture the violent torrent as I lounged in the gentle calm flow just below the dam and looked upstream at a dry wall of concrete, not a cascade of mud and logs. If I'd been there on June 24, 1972, I would have been killed.

Two mature eagles launched from a water willow bed in the middle of the river. An immature one took off from the top of a river maple on the shore. The birds wouldn't have been there in 1972 either. They were too rare. The insecticides, DDT, and DDE caused eagle egg shells to thin, which meant the eggs cracked before hatching and the national symbol was almost driven to extinction.

National environmental legislation such as the National Environmental Policy Act, the Clean Water Act, and the Federal Pesticide Control Act, which protected the eagles, all came right around the time of Hurricane Agnes. Before then it had been accepted practice to dump everything into our waters. Hazardous waste and raw sewage went into our rivers untreated. No wonder our rivers were dying, and a natural disturbance, like a hurricane, almost killed the Chesapeake Bay. It was already weakened from everything we'd done to it.

Water quality has improved as a result of the regulations passed in the early 70s, but we still struggle with too much nitrogen and sediment entering our rivers. Fish haven't done as well. The Maryland darter and hellbender salamander were last seen in this area in the late 80s and are expected to be gone. New arrivals assure a changed ecology. If hellbenders were here, I don't see how they could survive the gaping predatory mouths of flathead catfish, which are native to most of the Mississippi drainage, but are introduced here. The fates of the hellbenders and darters were probably sealed long before the flatheads arrived. Shad are holding at historically low levels. The Susquehanna was a world class smallmouth bass fishery just a few years ago, but now the Susquehanna smallmouths are in trouble. Males have been found with ovaries and other smallies are turning up with lesions. No one can agree on a cause so there is no progress toward a solution. Our rivers are never safe and secure from the damage we inflict. Conditions change and river ecology suffers.

I looked for fish that were still in the lower Susquehanna rather than the ones we might have lost. There is still an amazing system there. The architecture of smoothed, huge bedrock outcroppings that characterize that part of the river always gives an otherworldly feel. I started to see water willow rhizomes as I pulled myself along the bottom so I knew I was approaching an island or sand bar. Young fish used the protection of water willow stands and two juvenile log perch foraged on the bottom between the green shoots. Their tiger striping is always dramatic. Darters flitted around and a school of some kind of minnow turned in unison. Power in numbers.

And at one time there was power in environmental laws. We made great strides in protecting our rivers in the era of environmental regulation. The problems our rivers face today are largely created by each one of us rather than single large polluters. Non-point sources of pollution, pollution that doesn't enter the river from the end of a pipe but rather operates more insidiously by coming from multiple sources, is much harder to control with regulation. There's a place for regulation, but there's a growing place for personal action. It's not time to get complacent. It's time to act. Every positive action matters and every negative action matters, regardless of how small. They all add up.

A few months later I suited up under the green branches of a hemlock tree while a faint mist rose off the water of this remote stream in the mountains of western Maryland, about as far as you can get from the lower Susquehanna and still be in Maryland. About as different as you can get in terms of surrounding land use. This stream was in the forest covered mountains of western Maryland. There were patches of snow on the ground under a thick hemlock canopy that were slowly melting in the 40 degree drizzle. I slid into the creek. A plastic wrapper flapped in the current, like a leaf pinned against a rock. It annoyed me. I found garbage even in that pristine mountain stream, at least as pristine as they come around there. I tried to ignore it, but I couldn't swim past it. I just wanted to watch the trout and sculpin, but could see the purple and silver wrapper flutter in my peripheral vision.

I usually pick stuff up when I snorkel. Makes me feel better. I have a hard time leaving crap there that doesn't belong. It's a small positive step I can take toward restoring our rivers and streams. I know there are larger issues than litter facing our surface waters: sedimentation, eutrophication or over-fertilization, exotic species invasions, serious threats from fracking and mining. And sometimes it feels like there isn't a whole lot I can do about those other things, while in fact there are. I can drive less, which produces less nitrogen, one of the major nutrients that causes eutrophication. I can control the runoff coming from my roof top and driveway by installing rain gardens and barrels. I can make sure I'm not serving as a vector for exotic species. I can reduce my energy footprint and I can support organizations like river advocacy organizations. But it's hard for me to see the direct results of these actions and so the satisfaction isn't always there. Removing trash provides the instant gratification and the hope I need to know that we can all make the word a better place.

I snagged the wrapper and continued on my exploration of this creek. I looked toward an undercut bank with a good amount of woody structure hanging into the hole. Excellent habitat for trout. Instead I found plastic tangled in the branches and roots of a hemlock. I snorkeled into the hole and removed the trash.

I saw some young trout and an amazingly colorful sculpin on this trip. These fish made the experience memorable. But what really impacted me was the empowerment that came from removing a few pieces of trash from the beautiful creek, and how those actions can translate into others that will also protect our rivers and streams.

Get out there, enjoy your local creek, and take a few steps to protect it. Whether that means driving less, getting involved in issues that affect it, or even just picking up a few pieces of garbage. It all adds up, and it all matters. A lot has changed since Agnes roared through 41 years ago. Some changes have helped to restore our rivers, some changes have had the opposite effect. Let's work so that a river snorkeler exploring this spot in 41 years can see clear progress.

4. Migration

Eels

I reached the new bank of Basin Run, a small tributary to the lower Susquehanna. The usual one was four feet underwater, which ran fast and full of sediment. It had been raining all day and the creek was just cresting its bank. I wouldn't be able to see anything underwater even if I could manage to keep from getting swept downstream. As badly as I wanted to get in, conditions were just too dangerous. I'd come on a rainy October night to witness a mass nocturnal migration of eels, but would have to miss it.

Eels used to be the most abundant fish in the Chesapeake watershed. Maybe they still are, but their numbers are declining. They live for about 25 years in the creeks, rivers, and streams throughout the watershed. For some still unknown reason, a portion of the population stops feeding and migrates downstream on dark nights with rising water around Halloween. The migrating eels go through incredible physiologic changes as they move toward the ocean: they don't eat, their eyes grow large, their pigmentation changes, they become sexually mature, and their physiology, used to handling the pressures of living in a freshwater environment, changes to handle the opposite pressures of living in an ocean environment.

All of these eels head to the Sargasso Sea, a part of the Atlantic that basically lies under the Bermuda triangle to spawn. Young eels emerge, ride ocean currents, and swim back up our rivers and creeks. Eel numbers have been declining since the 1980s, probably due to a combination of causes. Eels prefer to live in clean gravel and cobble bottomed streams. More and more of our stream bottoms are becoming choked with sediments due to farming, construction, and urbanization of their watersheds. Dams impede eel migration, especially the young eels returning to their rivers. One researcher found 10,000 baby eels per day trying to make their way back upstream at the base of a hundred foot dam in the Susquehanna River.

I'm connected to these fish. My relatives used to build eel weirs in the Susquehanna to trap them during their migration. An eel weir is essentially a V-shaped dam made from piled rocks that points downstream. It's open at the apex and the migrating eels swim through that opening into waiting baskets. It's a technology Europeans learned from Native Americans. The remnants of one of my family's weirs can still be seen in the Susquehanna near the Swatara Creek. Swatara is derived from the Susquehannock word *swahadowry*, which means "where we feed on eels."

There's a picture in a family photo album of me holding an eel on the end of my fishing line, and that picture captures one of my first memories fishing. One of the best dives I ever experienced was with my dad and eels in the Delaware River. We entered at night between Easton, PA and Phillipsburg, NJ. We descended to the bottom of the river 20 feet below in clear water and found ourselves in a field of eels that stuck half of their bodies out of their burrows and slowly waved back and forth in unison in the gentle current, the way a hay field undulates in a breeze.

Eels are a fish I see regularly when I snorkel, and one section of Deer Creek seems to always hold a lot. One spring they were late to emerge, and I was getting worried. I'd been waiting for them. The spring before I couldn't snorkel Deer Creek without seeing at least a half dozen. Eels might be the most abundant fish in the Chesapeake watershed, but they are secretive and largely nocturnal so they aren't as obvious as the less abundant but more visible fish species.

I don't know why they are attracted to this rapid. It's not the easiest place to swim. The water is fast and turbulent, so I didn't expect to see a fish that slithers more than swims hunting there. But in years past, there they were, in the middle of the rapid, poking their heads into the nooks and crannies of the boulder bottom, looking for a morsel to eat. They were usually so intent on the hunt, I often went unnoticed. As I watched, their use of the rapid started to make sense. Their bodies are perfectly shaped to hug the crags on the bottom largely out of the flow. Their slim shape allows them to probe the depths of each potential fish hiding spot. When they finally recognized me, they slithered along the bottom, fighting the current, and disappeared. I wondered how many eels lived in the rapid. It's one of the fish I expect to see on each visit spring summer and fall.

But this year, I hadn't seen the fish in that rapid yet and spring was progressing. I hoped they were present. It's a strange thing, knowing that rivers and streams change. Knowing that the life that is there changes too. Unfortunately, most of the change that happens in our rivers and streams occurs at our hands, so when one of the members of the fish community doesn't return the next year, I worry that something happened to eliminate them. I worried that the eels in Deer Creek were gone.

I slid into the rapid and hung on as usual. The water wanted to peel me off the rock I was clawing and throw me downstream. I darted into an eddy that gave a little protection from the strong flow, and inched upstream to the downstream side of the large boulder that formed the eddy.

I didn't see anything. The spot usually produced at least one eel each trip but there was nothing. Finally, I saw some motion on the bottom. A young eel probed the crevices between rocks. It didn't even acknowledge my presence. A second juvenile hunted in the main part of the current. I was relieved to see those fish. All was right with the world. I have a lot of concern for the future health of our rivers and streams. And seeing fish return to their springtime place in the river gives me hope.

I've seen the spring return of juvenile eels to our streams over a number of years. But I still haven't witnessed the fall adult downstream mass migration. I want to swim downstream with the eels, to get their perspective on at least the beginning of their journey. My concern was that since I had always missed the event, I might have missed the last chance. But I would be back next year in October on a dark night with rising water to see if I could swim with the eels.

Circle of Life

I'd been checking Principio Creek daily for the last two months, anxiously waiting for the return of the herring. The Department of Natural Resources sign nailed to a tree was not a good omen, but I thought it was more preventive in nature. Possession of any herring, unless you had a receipt to prove you bought it last year, was now illegal due to a 93% reduction in herring numbers on the Atlantic coast over last 25 years. But I really didn't think that 93% reduction applied to the creek. The run last year had been incredibly abundant, so abundant that it had been easy to think it would continue.

Herring are migratory. They spend the majority of their lives at sea and migrate to our freshwater rivers and streams to spawn each spring. That same time the previous year I'd shared the base of Principio Falls with three fishermen who were trying to snag the migrants for bait. I watched thousands of fish push up through the falls. I watched thousands of fish lay and fertilize eggs.

I left Principio confident in the future of the herring run and looked forward to the opportunity to witness one of the most amazing events in our rivers and streams every spring. But the fish never came back and every day I checked, I came away wondering if I was early or they were late, but I figured they would be back. They had to. There were so many of them last year. It was a seasonal rite of passage I was confident I could hand down to my kids, maybe even my grandkids. It was something in nature I could count on returning. Until that moment. The first week of May arrived without sighting any herring and I had to accept that they weren't coming back that year.

It seemed like such a limitless resource, and while I'm not a proponent of overfishing, I didn't think the fishermen last year had been doing any harm. There were just so many fish in the creek, how could the couple dozen they removed have an effect? Nature would make more. Maybe that's why we are where we are, because of that very flawed thinking that our resources are so abundant we can never deplete them.

The lack of a run in the Principio was concerning, especially combined with a 93% reduction in Mid-Atlantic seaboard herring. Maybe the Prinicipio run was gone for good and all that remains are the pictures I took last year of the last run. Or maybe the warm and dry weather we had reduced all the runs. Sure seemed like the Deer Creek shad run fizzled after a robust start. I hoped it was the weather.

One year later, I stood on the bedrock that overlooks Principio Falls and hoped for herring. I wanted to capture the fish in photos, not on stringers. I started counting days to their arrival long before the end of winter. I hoped their absence the previous year had been just an aberration and not indicative of the precipitous decline in their numbers. I hoped the Principio still had a herring run, and I had to wait an entire year for the chance to get into the water and see if the fish had returned.

I scanned the stair step waterfall pools for any sign of herring, and found none. If they were there, they weren't as abundant as in 2011. I suited up and slid into the water. There weren't any fish. Not even darters which had been abundant on almost every snorkel exploration there. I crawled upstream against a strong current, slid up a short falls, and dropped into the first pool. Initially, I just saw water clouded by algae fragments and fine entrained air bubbles, but then the first silver shape came just barely into view, then another. There were about six herring in the pool, where at least 50 held the last time I'd snorkeled with them. But six was better than the zero I'd seen the previous year. I floated and watched for a while, absorbing the sight. Six fish acted out on ancient instinct to get to clean freshwater gavel beds to spawn, to start the next generation of herring that would return to the river to start the next generation and so on. There was something immortal about the whole thing.

I ascended a three foot bedrock ledge, slipped into the next highest pool, and found more herring, acting with the same singleness of purpose to get up the falls to their spawning grounds. I felt better seeing this other dozen or so fish. Maybe the Principio herring run was intact. Maybe I would be able to share this incredible feat with my grandkids. Maybe I could pass that legacy on. There is something immortal about that too. I snapped photos as fast as the camera would allow.

I returned two weeks later hoping the run would be in full swing. An older gentleman stood by a pool a hundred yards downstream. He had a full gray beard, wore a dirty t-shirt and jeans and a worn baseball hat. He sipped on a beer while he looked into the water. I searched the pools closer to the falls. We were both looking for herring.

"See any?" I called over the roar of the river.

"Nope."

Silence fell between us as we watched the water.

"I remember when they were so thick, their backs broke the water; they was stacked on top of each other. But then this creek took a beating since then. Too much mud in the water."

He went on to tell me the seasonal nuances of the shad and herring runs, and the movements of other migrants in the creek, like eels. I could tell that he cared for this river very much, just like me, but he knew it much better.

I hoped the few herring that had been there two weeks prior had just been the start of a strong run for the river. I'd become distracted by a few other streams that were full of fish and had been snorkeling them over the past two weeks, so I hadn't seen if the trickle of fish had picked up into a good flow. It hadn't. I'd missed the amazing herring run this river used to host—fish so thick they bumped into me in the water as I watched their upriver procession.

Another river I snorkel regularly followed a similar pattern but a third had an incredibly abundant run that year. Regionally herring numbers have significantly declined in the Mid-Atlantic over the last few decades. I'm hopeful that the great runs will return, and as long as there are herring making their way upstream to spawn, there's promise.

The older man and I watched the water in silence, both of us wanted to see the splash of a tail or the flash of a side. Any sign that the fish were running upstream. There was nothing. I felt disappointed and very concerned. There had been more fish there that year than in the last, but that's wasn't saying much. And once again I had to wait a year to see if the run would return.

"It ain't nothin' o' what it used to be," my new friend said.

"No it's not," I replied. "But hopefully they'll come back."

"I hear they're running thick in the North East," he hollered over the water.

So I went there, to a pool at the base of the falls near the Amtrak bridge on the North East Creek. The last time I'd been in the North East I'd admired the alien stream scape of a significantly degraded creek just upstream of the falls. The bottom was a flat sand, mud, and gravel plane covered in tan and olive algae. Oxygen bubbles formed on the algae and added quicksilver highlights. Castle spire fronds of algae reached toward the surface where enough bubbles formed to provide lift.

The North East is pretty significantly degraded by sedimentation, eutrophication, over-fertilization that makes too much algae grow. Still, this section was interesting, messed up as it was. It was a nice place to visit once but there were many other streams for me to explore, so I'd never returned. Until now.

A thick furry growth of algae covered everything. I could see it from the surface and I wondered if the trip would be similar to my last: a swim over an interesting stream scape, but one that really didn't hold much diversity. Then a few tails slapped the surface as the fish struggled their way up through the rapid. The herring were there.

The bottom was angulated fractured bedrock and dropped to a four foot hole. The first fish I saw was a large log perch, large as far as log perch come. A school of some kind of medium-sized minnow swam upstream along the bottom. A few sunnies held in a corner of the deeper pool. A hefty eel hunted. I couldn't believe the diversity. In just a few minutes I saw a half dozen species of fish. Then the herring arrived. Schools of the silver fish swarmed around me in an energetic mating frenzy. Many of the shiny torpedoes swam into me. I'd never been swimming with so many fish.

The four foot hole grew dense with herring and a couple of shad. Herring and shad numbers have been tenuous over the last decades and seeing those fish was reassuring and should give us hope at a time when it seems all the news about the environment is negative. Hope that we can restore what we've degraded, and hope in the knowledge that even in their degraded states, our local rivers and streams are still pretty amazing places.

A few weeks later, the run was over. A shad lay on the bottom on its side and still passed water over its gills, but barely. Its body was a mottled dark purple and blue instead of clean silver. A sad sight, but the shad had run its course. This is the natural order. Shad migrate in the spring and some of them die in the process, unlike salmon where each migrant swims upstream to its death. Many shad return year after year to spawn. But this shad was one of the group that wouldn't be returning next year.

As I watched this fish work to pump water over its gills, I felt for this animal. It obviously wanted to live. It was struggling to survive even though it was such an obviously futile attempt. At the same time, its presence was a sign of hope. That shad are there at all is a miracle. The North East is a fairly impacted stream, and there is a short dam a half mile upstream just tall enough to stop shad from making their way any further up the river.

But the fish was there, which I assumed meant it made its way as far upstream as it could, laid its eggs, or fertilized some, and set the process in motion for future runs of shad. This fish lived the life it was supposed to live and it was now done. There shouldn't be anything sad about that, rather there should be joy and hope that we should all be so lucky.

I continued on over thick growths of stringy algae. But the sunnies didn't mind and as I floated into a large eddy to the side of a short riffle, I was greeted by curious small bluegill, and large defensive male pumpkin seeds in full red coloration. I stayed for as long as the cold water allowed, watching the blue gill get closer, and the pumpkin seeds take aggressive postures then swim off in a tight circle only to return nose to nose with me. A lot of these fish are non-native to the North East. Many species of sunfish were introduced there and they have become part of the natural aquatic backdrop. The algae don't belong there either, at least not in the quantities in which they're found. The only thing I saw that day that belonged in the North East was the dying shad. But even in that impacted stream there is something of worth and value to see. For the North East that's ancient migrations hanging on, and in some cases making a comeback, and non-native fish putting on incredible displays of color and territoriality.

The next spring I watched Deer Creek from the Shuresville Road bridge on Easter weekend. The water just upstream sporadically boiled as the early evening darkened. Must be shad, I thought, and after a few minutes of looking, confirmed my suspicion: the shad had arrived to spawn; their tails rapidly beat the shallow riffle into a boil. I needed to get into the water to witness this timeless rite from the perspective of these fish. Shad are in the herring family and are anadramous, meaning that, like salmon, they spend their lives at sea and endure an arduous spring journey as they swim inland to spawn in smaller creeks. Many shad are declining in number and some are endangered. Dams, which sever migration routes, and sediments, which cover gravel spawning beds, are the two current reasons for the ongoing lack of recovery. There aren't any dams between that stretch of Deer Creek and the Atlantic, so shad can make the 175 mile journey from the ocean to that riffle unimpeded by concrete walls. The fish returned, driven by the primal urge to ensure their immortality by passing their genes on to the next generation. I wanted to witness this incredible act.

I slipped into the water downstream of the shad and fought a heavy current. I didn't see any fish as I crawled my way against the flow. A fisherman from shore directed me to where the fish were spawning—a little further upstream and a little further out in the current. Ghostly blurs appeared on my periphery as shad shot past, then I felt a slap on my shoulder. I was right in the middle of the spawning school. I could barely hang onto the bottom against the current, and shad darted by with effortless but strong tail strokes. It was obvious their compressed bodies and powerful, deeply forked tails make them perfectly designed for the reproductive task at hand. Silver tails flashed over a particular spot in the stream bed just upstream as females released eggs and males released sperm, while fish continued to rush upstream. From above their olive backs made them invisible against the bottom. From beneath the surface, their silver bodies were obvious through the early spring's hazy water.

This was the first school of the year, maybe one hundred fish strong, that had made it to the swimming hole in Susquehanna State Park. There were a few yellow perch there too. The spring spawning migration of shad returning into our streams is a fraction of what it once was. And there are some species, like American shad, that are still struggling. Yellow perch, also recently declining in number, seemed to have reversed and their population is growing.

I celebrated these ecological victories as I floated in the pool above my favorite rapid and watched each individual struggle against the current to reach its clean gravel spawning ground. People recognized that shad were declining and decided to do something about it, so their return is a testament to what we can accomplish when we put our will behind action. It's a testament to the tenacity and resilience of ecological systems. There are definitely limits, and we can easily exceed them.

At the same time, there is elasticity, and if we recognize those limits early enough, and act, the system can recover. All is not lost. Not yet. But we need to act.

I figure shad have been making treks like that for 60 million years or so. And yet we might make them extinct in my lifetime. I feel fortunate to have experienced the timelessness of this event, timeless in relation to my fleeting human life span. Knowing these fish are there and spawning makes me believe more will follow, and that maybe the great mythic shad runs I've heard of that occurred before I was born may once again fill our streams.

It's fitting that shad returned on Easter weekend. It's a time of promise, resurrection, and rebirth, and their presence in the creek signals the continuation of their species, the optimism that more will return next year. More proof that maybe their species has been resurrected. It's one of the most hopeful events we can experience in our streams.

Seeing these first migrants makes me optimistic that that we will recognize the limits we are fast approaching, drop the rhetoric, and get busy. Seeing these fish renews my commitment to show people the incredible life just beneath the surface of our local streams.

I returned to the Principio the next spring. Blueback herring were holed up in pools of the Principio Falls, spawning, oblivious to me, the intruder. Masses of metallic blue and silver shot past upstream and swirled back downstream in pulsating eddies of fish. Their numbers had returned.

A dead half-eaten herring lay on the bottom on a bed of eggs. Eggs covered part of the carcass. The entire bottom was covered in eggs, and they occasionally swirled up past my face mask when an eddy whirled them back into the water column. Nothing goes to waste, and I was sure the rest of the herring would be eaten by something in the next few hours, giving sustenance to a heron, or otter, crayfish, or catfish. Just as I was sure most of the millions of eggs would become something else's dinner rather than become new blue-backed herring. It's hard to tell whose eggs are whose and who fertilized which ones. It's just one procreative soup, and each fish contributes with the hope and expectation that their young will make it, assuming that they achieved a form of immortality by passing their genetic information to the next generation.

The remains of the dead herring were a reminder that I would be there too someday, and the eggs were a reminder that my kids would be there to carry on. The amazing annual feat of migration, life and death, models the brevity of our journeys and the spiraling cycle of life.

That's Not a Shad

The shad had been running for a few weeks, and I was still in awe of their migration after being in the water with them a dozen times. Their spawning is the sign that I look for to tell me that spring is here.

Others had joined the shad since the first day of their journey. I watched carp swim with the shad and a large eel bisected a school in an eddy. The shad draw more humans as well, and available parking spaces became rarer as the shad run increased. Room on the river to snorkel between fishermen got a little tight. Herons and humans, shad and carp, all participate in this rite of seasonal passage.

But the spring migration had reached crescendo and was trickling away. There were fewer fishermen, more parking spots, and less fish. I was a little disappointed to see all the action and excitement of their incredible journey cease until next year. Witnessing the drama of the upstream push, and experiencing a little of it by swimming with the fish on the journey makes me feel alive.

Hundreds of hickory shad pushed their way upstream to spawn. I hovered on the edge of the current in a large eddy and stretched out into the stream to get as close to the school as possible without interrupting the procession.

The fish got used to me and allowed me to stay without leaving until I coughed, or cleared my leaky snorkel. They swam from the hole when they heard the noise and timidly returned a few minutes later. I just hung out with the fish, a part of an eons old ritual of upstream migration, and enjoyed the privilege of witnessing this feat. There was an intensity of purpose with the fish. There wasn't much that was going to keep them from their destination, and I absorbed as much of the view of their journey as I could.

The fish scattered and the pool became eerily still. There weren't silver tubes struggling upstream in the hazy distance. There weren't the lower jaws with overbites characteristic of hickory shad, wiggling side to side in the current. There was an unexplained quiet in the pool and I thought I saw a large shadow pass just barely out of sight. If I were in the ocean I would have been thinking *predator* from the way the fish disappeared when a shadow appeared. But this was a freshwater stream, and I figured my imagination was at work. The shad returned and I went back to enjoying their activity.

Then it happened again. The shad scattered, the pool became still, and I had a creepy feeling that something big was moving just out of view. Then I saw it—a large shadowy shape coming up through the middle of the rapid on the bottom. Then another came into hazy view and another. There was a school of them, whatever they were.

As they came further upstream, closer to me, I could make out some features. The fish were two feet long and rotund. They looked too big to be there, in the swift moving water. Shad are compressed side to side with deeply forked tails that propel them upstream through strong downstream currents, and these fish were much too tubular and less hydrodynamic to make such a journey. But there they were. I thought they were carp at first, but then saw they didn't have any barbels, which are whisker like sensory organs near the mouth that help the fish search for food in murky water, and the front edge of their dorsal fin extended into a long thread or quill, which gives them their name: Quillback.

Quillback are another migrant in our rivers and streams. Whereas shad migrate hundreds if not thousands of miles, Quillback cover shorter distances. They spend most of their lives in larger rivers and migrate into smaller streams to spawn. They were looking for the same thing as shad: clean gravel beds. It was a true thrill to hold on to the bottom in the middle of six of these foot and a half long fish. They seemed to acknowledge and accept my presence and kept on pumping their caudal fins against the current, right next to me, so that I could feel the pressure waves coming off their tails through my wetsuit.

I've been around for almost 50 years and am still learning about our rivers and streams. I never knew quillback traveled upstream in search of gravel beds to spawn. I never really looked for them. Learning like this makes life exciting.

Quillback have become one of the species I look for in spring as part of the migration. I went snorkeling in the Octoraro Creek, near where it empties into the Susquehanna. It was a celebration as hundreds of herring and shad streamed past me. The Octoraro's run had been weak of late, but the run this year looked pretty good. The water was clear and I enjoyed being in the moment, watching. I drifted over a six foot deep pool and found that the bottom was whipped into a flocculent cloud. Large metallic powder blue sparks flashed through the clouded haze. It was like watching a lightning storm from above. Bolts of glowing blue shot through the water. I dived to the bottom and watched quillback rocket around in circles in this deeper pool, trying to attract a mate with pectoral fin flashes. The fish knew I was there but had other more important things on their minds and they swirled around in hap hazard patterns. The pool was a chaos of fish, and I was in the middle of it all.

A few weeks later I walked across the dry riverbed of the Susquehanna just below the Holtwood Dam. The scene looked more like the Serengeti than the Susquehanna. A wide open area of green water willow grassland was interspersed with an occasional tree that had survived the seasonal torrents. Large expanses of bedrock, whitewashed with dried biofilm, reflected the sun's heat and reminded me of hiking over a salt flat.

I reached the edge of a hundred yard long pool that was effectively severed from the main flow of the river. I geared up with my back to the pool and heard a large splash. I turned but didn't see anything. Nothing moved after watching the water for a few minutes. I went back to putting on my wetsuit and heard another one. What was making these splashes?

The water in the pool was dark compared to the brightness of the exposed flat bedrock. Dark green algae covered everything and absorbed much of the light. The bottom of the pool was angulated bedrock that dropped into deep narrow ravines. The water was murky with churned up bottom, a sign that something big was in the pool with me. I came upon two good sized small mouth bass showing off for each other, part of the mating dance, and I figured that was what had caused the splashes and churned bottom. But still, I was nervous. The bass just weren't big enough to account for all that noise. Suddenly, a big school of huge quillback burst past me. Some of the fish bumped into me in their eagerness to mate and escape. I felt like I was swimming through the buffalo stampede scene in *Dances with Wolves*. The school felt like it was a hundred strong, but it could have been the same 25 fish over and over, blowing by me, running into me, darting to and from every direction. Some of them came so close I could touch them with my nose, and their big scales became apparent. I couldn't track them or predict where the next one was coming from. They each had such a strength about them, such an incredible amount of life, and all or nothing attitude. The school swarmed and circled and darted and as fast as they arrived, they were gone and the pool sat still and clouded.

Our rivers and streams burst with biologic power in spring and early summer. There is so much energy, excitement, and drama in the quest to produce the next generation. And I got to witness and experience the struggle to ensure the survival of the species simply by snorkeling my local stream.

5. Fish

Mouth with a Tail

There wasn't much going on in Deer Creek in terms of fish. Nothing was moving and I didn't see anything between the cobbles besides a few caddisflies. The water was fast and hazy due to recent rains and I was just about to get out. I traversed the hard current across a set of riffles just to enjoy the rush of water and the feeling of flying one more time when two large green eyes peered back at me from between two rocks on the bottom. The sight startled me. I wasn't sure what animal they belonged to. Once I realized they weren't moving but just watching me, I crept in for a closer look. I saw a huge downturned mouth on a large head, attached to a small tail in comparison. This was a sculpin. They look like tadpoles with a big head relative to the skinnier tail, kind of like a giant comma.

Sculpins live on the bottom and are ambush predators. They are amazingly camouflaged to blend in with their surroundings and patiently wait for insects or other fish to wander by. Their face is dominated by a huge mouth which they whip open to suck in unsuspecting prey. Smaller sculpin eat mayflies, while larger ones eat caddisflies, crayfish, and worms. Smaller sculpins are often eaten by larger ones. A common belief among trout fishermen is that sculpins eat trout eggs but studies have shown that trout eat sculpins, and sculpin fly patterns are popular with fly fishermen.

I decided to check out a small tributary a little further upstream. New cobbled riffles had formed beneath a large beaver controlled pool, due to a rearrangement of a beaver dam that had scoured the finer particles from the larger rock. I wasn't there for more than a minute before a northern hog sucker sped downstream and disappeared into a collection of leaves and beaver chews hung up on the bank. I looked for the fish in the tangle, and noticed a sculpin looking back at me from the gravel bottom.

I knew sculpins should be there, but have never seen any, and for as many times as I have been in Big Branch, I was starting to wonder if maybe the bottom was just too sandy to support sculpins. But they are dominant in that gravelly stretch so I saw another and another. A fourth and fifth hung out together for a while, but then they too dissolved into the background as soon as I took my eye off them. The juvenile sculpin stand a good chance of being eaten by a trout or another sculpin.

A male sculpin staked out a cavity under a rock and swam out short distances to entice an egg laden female into his lair where they turned upside down, pressed their abdomens to the ceiling of the male's newly constructed home, and stuck fertilized eggs to the roof of the void. The female swam away shortly after (males eat smaller females) and the male stayed with the eggs to fan them, which would keep them silt free. Sculpin eggs don't do well in sediment.

A few months later, I slipped into another Pennsylvania mountain stream that must have been sediment choked a century ago, during the heyday of the Pennsylvania lumber boom when forests were clear cut and soils flowed into our streams. This visit was much different, and what was a silted in pool 100 years ago was now a pool lined in clean granite rock.

A sculpin emerged from the background that closely matched the fish's camouflage. The river had been restored but that didn't mean there weren't any threats. While sculpin are common right now, nothing is guaranteed forever. A new threat could emerge and wipe them out. I never take anything for granted in our streams, no matter how common a species is, so I spend the afternoon watching, admiring, and appreciating the fish that are all mouths with tails hop from nook to cranny as they hunt for food in a currently clean stream.

Sunny Entertainment

The Brandywine at the Stroud Preserve has a diversity of habitats: slow moving areas with sandy/silty bottoms, underwater vegetation beds, cobble flats where the river picks up speed, woody shoreline debris, shallow riffles, and scour holes. The diversity of habitats should provide a diversity of fish, and I expected to see a ton as I slid into the river near the downstream riffle. The reflection on the smooth surface rippled as I pushed off the shore.

I dug my fingers into the soft bottom to claw my way upstream. While the river was calm, it was still moving. I drifted past underwater vegetation beds interspersed with sand and gravel flats and saw no fish. I slid over cobble piles and saw no fish. The river bottom dropped off into deeper holes and still no fish. I started to doubt whether I would see anything on the trip. That's how it goes sometimes. Sometimes river snorkeling is more about enjoying the underwater river scape, enjoying the river from a very different perspective. I continued upstream, and looked for sunnies.

I can always count on sunnies just about anywhere I snorkel in spring, summer, and fall. They are everywhere and while they are a common fish, their behavior is always interesting and enjoyable to watch. I headed for the woody debris near the shoreline and coasted under the bridge. There, blending in really well to the backdrop of sticks and silt, was a school of a half dozen sunnies intently watching my every move.

Sunny is a generic term applied to members of the sunfish family that includes 28 species. Some of these hybridize readily which can make getting a positive ID difficult. A few of the fish there were pumpkinseeds, a species of sunny. They are the fish familiar to most kids who go fishing.

Pumpkinseeds are beautiful fish with deep yellow orange undersides, metallic sky blue lines that run through a reddish orange flecked field on their heads and gill covers, red eyes, and black, white, orange, and yellow flecked sides.

Pumpkinseeds are generalists and eat an assortment of insects, snails, crustaceans and fish. They feed at all levels in the water column and are effective predators on mosquito larvae. They have fine gill rakers that look like small combs on the gills which enable them to filter small food particles from the water. All predators eat juvenile pumpkinseeds, including the adults of their own species.

But I really didn't care about the exact identity of the species in front of me. Rather, I enjoyed watching their behavior: how they responded to me, the river, and the other sunnies.

The bottom of that stretch of river was dotted with bowl shaped nests the males had constructed, and they got right in my facemask to defend their territory. Others darted after males who wandered into their turf. I settled into watching a large male who held his ground against me, an organism hundreds of times larger; a demonstration of their tenacity. I moved my head to the left and he stayed nose to nose. I moved to the right; he moved to the right. It looked like his breast turned redder the longer I stayed and his motions grew more aggressive toward me.

Males swam out from their nests to entice a female in. Successful males swim in a tight circle side by side with the female as she lies over on one side. The female releases her eggs as the male releases his milt or sperm and the fertilized eggs fall into the bowl of the nest. The males continue to defend the nest even after the eggs hatch and they have been known to scoop up wandering fry in their mouths to return them to the nest. Pumpkinseeds have a strong homing ability as well. Pumpkinseeds that were relocated to other parts of lakes were able to return to where they were originally captured.

A small mouth bass patrolled around me, careful to keep me in sight as I drifted with the current. A juvenile bass darted for the opposite shore. I could see the ghostly outlines of large river chubs in the bottom of a deeper hole. Common shiners fed on the morsels I inadvertently kicked off the bottom, and darters lay among the gravel, ready to pounce. Even if I hadn't seen the other fish that represent the diversity I'd first expected, it still would have been an amazing trip. Sunnies always entertain.

Darting Rainbows

There were hundreds of darters at Principio Falls. The darters had been there for a few weeks, and I figured they were congregating to mate, but they were just starting to display breeding behavior. Males were in breeding color and fanned their fins to attract a mate, advertising they were the most fit based on their dorsal fin. Maybe size does matter. Either way, watching the males display and females respond was entertaining.

They were even in the falls themselves, right at the fall line where the Principio tumbles 30 feet over bedrock. I am always amazed at how such a dainty looking fish like a darter can hang on in such intense conditions. I hopped from waterfall pool to waterfall pool, and came upon a three foot fissure. There were darters there, of course.

A large fish floated under me as I admired the darters' ability to wriggle into cracks and flatten to the bedrock to hold in the mid-waterfall pool. As much as I didn't expect a few inch long darters to be there they weren't a shock. Foot long suckers were. The first one took off when it realized it had just drifted under something much larger. I followed the fissure, barely a foot wide and found the rest of the sucker school. I couldn't believe that many large, lumbering fish could make a living in the intense currents of a waterfall.

I'd really expected the pool to be devoid of life simply because of the intense physical conditions. Consistently strong currents, heavy, scouring flows with almost every runoff producing rain, and not many places to hide due to the smooth bedrock nature of the bottom, aren't very conducive for fish to survive. And yet there was an entire community living in the mid-waterfall pool.

Darters were relegated to the nooks and crannies of smooth bedrock walls in what I think was an example of habitat partitioning. In colder months, when the minnows like common shiner are less common, darters dominate the whole stream. In warmer months, when other competitors increase their numbers, the darters switch to bedrock where they are better adapted to survive. At least that's my theory.

Juvenile darters hopped from cranny to cranny just like the adults. One of the things I love about the spot is watching darter courtship displays in the spring. I got to watch the result of that effort and it's reassuring to know they will continue.

The darters living here are the common johnny and tessellated darters, though I have a hard time differentiating the two if I don't have them in a net. Most fish have a swim bladder, a gas filled chamber that helps control their buoyancy. Darters don't, and their tails are rounded, which makes them inefficient swimmers, so they spend most of their time on the bottom and move from place to place in short hops or "darts." Male tesselateds' dorsal fins darken and I've seen them take on a magenta hue in spring, when they acquire breeding color. Males choose spawning sites under overhanging logs or rocks and guard their spot. When a male sees a gravid female he initially aggressively approaches her with a fins erect threatening display. If she doesn't swim away, he tries to lure her into his nest.

Either fish initiates spawning by turning upside down with their stomach against the roof of the den. The other fish follows along and the eggs are released, fertilized, and stuck to the roof of the nest. Males guard the nest and care for the eggs by swimming upside down over the eggs with their pelvic fins gently brushing over them. There are 166 species of darter in North America, and new species are still being discovered. They include some of the most ornately colored fish on the planet.

A few months later I was snorkeling on the New River in Virginia. Just as I was packing up at New River Junction, Jeremy Monroe, Director of *Freshwaters Illustrated* called me to finalize our plans for the rest of the week. I was joining Jeremy and the film crew from *Freshwaters Illustrated* as they completed work on a movie about the freshwater biodiversity of the Southeastern US. I develop curriculum to accompany many of Jeremy's movies, and I hoped to do the same for this effort. When Jeremy learned I was camping on the New River, he gave me a tip for a riffle that held candy darters, located in the Jefferson National Forest North of Pembroke, VA. I wasn't planning on snorkeling in Jefferson National Forest, but I couldn't pass up the possibility of seeing candy darters. I've seen pictures of these fish in field guides and wondered if the artists' renderings were more fiction than fact. I didn't think fish that brightly colored—red, orange, green, and turquoise—were supposed to live in North America.

The riffle didn't look like much from the surface. Not much more than shin deep. But as soon as I stuck my face in the water, a candy darter shot off. The fish was just as brightly colored as the field guide illustrations. They weren't artistic exaggerations. The candy darter had orange undersides with orange bands outlined in white against a turquoise background on its body. Its aquamarine fins were fringed with orange. It looked like someone had constructed a fish out of colorful playdough and placed it in this stream, until it shot off. Another darted from behind a rock and I was able to slowly trail it upstream and snap multiple shots of the amazingly colored fish.

The most ornately colored darter that lives in the streams I snorkel regularly is the green darter. Green-sided darters are elusive. I have unsuccessfully chased them for weeks in Conowingo Creek just for the chance at a picture. I usually see them as dark green squiggles that quickly disappear somewhere into the bottom. They often look like algae blowing in the current. One spring I hunted for them on the Brandywine River just outside of Wilmington Delaware.

A dark green smudge darted across the gravel flat as soon as I stuck my face in the water of the Brandywine at the Natural Lands Trust Stroud preserve. I barely saw it so a positive identification wasn't possible but based on the little that I had seen—dark green color, robust but small body, and fast bottom swimming—I was sure it had been a green darter. I hoped it was a green darter. The males get brilliant emerald green vertical stripes in spring and early summer. I really wanted to see this fish, and maybe get a picture of it if I was lucky so I searched the flat gravel bottom for 15 minutes, and didn't see a thing. Not even other fish. Maybe seeing the possible green darter had been wishful thinking.

Green darters are one of those fish that, when in breeding color, don't look like they belong in this area. They look tropical, like I should see them in the Amazon basin somewhere, or maybe the

Congo. But they are in the Little Conestoga, and I was determined to find one.

The little Conestoga doesn't look like much, even under the surface. The water is milky and string bands of dark green algae latch onto twigs and rocks and billow downstream. I didn't see any fish at first. Then I thought I saw some movement, but it must have been the algae. Then I saw it again and a fish emerged into focus from the background. Finally, I was able to decipher their flowing algae camouflage and recognized a green darter before it disappeared so I could follow the fish and capture a photo of the elusive beauties. The fish looked smug, if darters could assume such an appearance. He held his head up high, snout up, and his mouth edges were downturned in a perpetual haughty pout. Emerald green bands streaked up and down on his body against a dusky yellow background. He sat stoutly crossways to the current with his fins waving in the current until he finally swam off and disappeared into the background. I floated back downstream.

The skittish river chub outswam me, but the tessellated darters were more reluctant to swim from their protective stones, so they tolerated my close approach. As common as they are tessellateds still hold my attention and fascination. I love how their bodies just kind of limply conform to the cobbles, and when I think the river is just pushing them around, they muster an incredible burst of energy and master the current to put distance between me and them. I love how their large pectoral fins, an almost iridescent blue, hold them to the bottom , and I love how some allow my camera to get within inches, while others scatter when I'm still a few feet away. I love that I get to see rainbows dart across the bottom.

Nothing Common about the Common

I dug the toes of my wetsuit boots into the rocky bottom as I struggled to keep my position in the current. It was hard to hold the camera broad to the flow with one hand, and every time I let go of the rocky bottom with the other to help stabilize the camera, the current turned my body sideways and forced me down stream. Yet the fish I was working so hard to photograph held their position without much more than a few flicks of their tails.

I finally pushed myself upstream, flowed back down partly through the beginning of the riffle and wedged myself, feet upstream, between two large rocks. This gave me a great vantage from which to watch the fish dart through the current to pluck whatever morsels of food flowed downstream. My feet took the brunt of the buffeting which freed my hands to work the camera. I swore I watched something beyond the ordinary—shad, or at least river herring. The way those fish darted through the current with the greatest agility to grab whatever my presence forced into the drift—that component of the creek's food supply, composed largely of insects that floated in mid-water column. They picked off whatever I rubbed from the bottom as my hands and feet grappled to hold my position in the creek, and whatever the stronger current—forced to the bottom beneath me—scoured from the rocks below.

Surely their bodies were built to migrate upstream long distances with such grace, something like a shad, or other migratory fish in the herring family. Their body shape was a little more rotund than the characteristic thin herring body form, but their aquatic dexterity surely put them in the same group as those great upstream migrants.

I was disappointed when a biologist friend confirmed their identity from one of my pictures as common shiners. Nothing more than common shiners. The same fish I've captured in nets and traps from creeks from all over the Mid-Atlantic for more than 30 years. I didn't think there was anything particularly special about these common fish. Not until I witnessed their swimming prowess in that riffle. All of my experience with shiners had taken place on my turf, in my dry element, on my terms. This was the first time I'd watched them in theirs, and my perception of them has been forever changed.

These aren't the clunky nondescript, unexciting silvery tubes flopping in the gut of a seine net anymore. They are fascinating, accomplished swimmers. I find this often, that aquatic organisms that are written off as common or ordinary, and mundane when we view them in air are fascinating in their own wet element.

Black-nosed dace are common fish, distributed throughout New England, west through the Great Lakes, and south through Tennessee, northern Georgia, and Alabama. They even occupy the most urban streams. They are mistakenly called shiners by most, though I knew them as stripers when I was catching them as a kid in the suburbanized Pumpkin Patch Creek. They were interesting fish as they flopped in the bottom of my net, their silver side bisected with a distinct clean black line.

In water, these fish are vibrant and thoroughly alive. They are fast and agile. While their colors were crisp out of the water in my net, in water their colors are more complex; a silver body with a black stripe out of water becomes metallic gold above and silver below in water. Males get orange fins in breeding season that glow against their gold, black, and silver bodies. All of these subtleties of color are lost out of water.

There are 127 species of fish called shiners in North America, and it's often hard to differentiate one species from the next. Most of them are some sort of minnow, which is a real family of fish called "cyprinids." But the common, nondescript name "shiner" is given to just about any fish that glistens a little and most fish that are used as bait. Some of the most intense battles I've witnessed in the fish world were between male shiners defending breeding territory. I've seen amazing examples of this in the Conasauga River, Tennessee.

The Conasauga houses one of the most diverse fish communities in the world. Its waters are clear thanks to its forested watershed in Cherokee National Forest. I was there with Casper Cox, a river snorkeling, native freshwater fish advocate and pioneer. I pulled my way up to the end of a rapid section where Casper had placed himself feet into the current and just watched the fish play out before him. Casper was great at picking a spot and just watching. I call him the "fish whisperer" because he uses his thorough knowledge of fish behavior to attract fish to him.

"Look here," Casper said. "There are two male Alabama shiners duking it out."

Just downstream from us two male Alabama shiners fought the current as they head bumped each other out of place in the stream. Male Alabama shiners, like many male minnows, grow bony bumps called "tubercles" on their heads in the mating season. The exact purpose of tubercles isn't known, but they seem to be used to help males spar like this.

These two males went at each other repeatedly. First one bumped the other out of place, followed by the displaced shiner regaining his spot, then the second bumped back. This went on until Casper spotted a few tricolor shiner males doing the same thing. He had one male taking on the end of a pointer stick Casper wiggled just in front of him to get the male to throw up his dorsal fin like a red, black, and white banded flag.

The iridescent powder blue tubercles on the Alabama shiner, and the red, black, and white dorsal fin on the tricolor, are examples of how male minnows experience some of the most drastic color changes in the animal kingdom in the breeding season. Species that are drab the rest of the year turn painted in order to attract mates.

My time with Casper and the Conasauga were up and I reluctantly returned home to less clear water. The first creek I snorkeled after I returned was Deer Creek, and I had to feel my way through it after April showers made the water turbid. I was about to get out. I couldn't see more than a foot in front of me. I traversed a powerful riffle and came up on a gravelly section of the river. A school of common shiner in breeding color danced in the current. They were unrecognizable compared to their usual coloration. Their pectoral fins were pastel orange and yellow, their bodies iridescent red. The males held against the strong current and slammed each other out of the way to claim the prime breeding spot and to attract a female.

Sometimes it's the color that amazes, sometimes it's the volume of fish. I once encountered a huge school of spot tail shiner where a stream emptied into a lake. As soon as I entered the water, I was in the midst of a thousand strong school of spot tail shiners, holding at a confluence of moving and still waters. These are common fish, and nondescript. They don't have elaborate fins or brilliant colors. They are easily overlooked, mundane. Their only distinguishing characteristic is a dark spot on their tails, thus the name spottail shiner.

But seeing thousands of the fish shoaled up was nothing short of remarkable. Why were they all there? Were they congregating to spawn? Or were they taking advantage of food flowing into Long Level from Fishing Creek?

Spottails are considered unimportant. No one catches them and only a handful of people realize they even exist. But swimming with these fish was like moving through a school of fish holding on the Great Barrier Reef; they were that abundant and moved in choreographed unison.

Just because they aren't economically important or noticed doesn't make them less valuable. All fish serve important roles in the ecology of our rivers and streams. Watching them live in their element helps highlight that importance. There's nothing common about the common.

The Joy of Trout

I slid into the cold clear water of Fishing Creek to scope it out for a trip I would be running. The architecture of the place instantly impressed. Water cascaded over shelves of schist bedrock into pools lined with smoothed bedrock and angulated slabs. The clarity was impressive.

I saw a group of minnows and crept in to try to get a good shot and positive identification. I noticed the speckled snout of a trout sticking out from under a rock. I pointed the camera at the trout and the fish allowed me to snap a few shots before it rocketed off into the main flow below a short falls, leaving the minnows in a cloud of silt.

I've always admired trout. They are elusive, and when I spent more time fishing for them than snorkeling with them, it was one of the ultimate challenges to hook one. Trout have an intelligence that makes it difficult to capture them. And now that I try to observe them, I find that they are just as difficult to watch.

My little trout shot off and joined another larger fish feeding in a deeper, swift current. I hid behind a rock and watched the two fish feed. They plucked insect morsels from the water with precise movements, maintaining position in the river. Watching them was like watching the most incredible ballet. They exemplified grace, power, agility.

It didn't take the fish long to realize they were being watched and they disappeared. I swam through the pool, but the only thing I found was a puff of sediment in a bedrock crevasse where one of the trout had hidden and shot off when I passed overhead. I caught peripheral glimpses of the fish through the rest of the trip, but wasn't able to spend any time watching them again. I enjoyed the beauty of Fishing Creek, looked for the trout, and admired their ability to dominate a pool one minute and completely vanish the next.

That was my relationship with trout for a long time. Until I found the Susquehanna Riverlands preserve streams protected by the Lancaster Conservancy. Tucquan Glenn is one of those and my experience with trout there started out similar to that of other streams.

I went in expecting to see a lot of fish, specifically trout. I had snorkeled Tucquan Creek a few summers ago. The water was muddy following some July showers, and the shadows of larger fish stayed in view just long enough for my imagination to identify them as native brook trout, but they never came close enough for me to confirm.

I returned on an early spring day when the water was clearer. Showers threatened as I suited up alongside the creek. Tucquan Creek looks and feels remote. It cascades over schist shelves through a steep-sided hemlock and rhododendron valley. The spring forest floor was covered in may apple, tooth wort, trout lily, and a few trillium. It's easy to imagine the eddies and holes filled with trout nose up in the current waiting to pluck insect morsels as they drift by. I expected to not only see these fish, but to capture their images since the last time I'd been there the murk made catching a shot of them impossible.

A tan shape shot from under a rock to under a short falls. Was it a trout? I crawled upstream toward a chute that cascades water over a one-foot falls. The environment there was otherworldly. It was loud. All I could hear was the rush of water that sounded like a train. Air bubbles blinded me. I pulled myself through the current to behind the chute and witnessed the force of the water as it carved smooth holes in the sparkly, silver-orange bedrock. I didn't see any fish. I drifted with the current back downstream, let myself experience the freedom of getting spun in an eddy, and looked under a lone rock in the middle to a pool. There, hidden in the shadow, was a brown trout that stared back at me for a second, then rocketed out of the pool with one powerful flick of its tail.

The next winter I returned after an ice storm glazed everything, including the forest floor. The mile hike in was tricky and I wished I'd worn crampons to navigate a few steep and slick sections. I crawled over the trail in a few places to keep from falling into the chasm the river carved through the bedrock 20 feet below. Most of the river was frozen over except where the water moved especially fast. The plunge pool below a five-foot falls had open water, so I got in there.

The water stung but was clear and I instantly saw two large brown trout lying on the bottom of the four-foot deep pool. They shot upstream into a void carved behind the waterfall as I slowly drifted over them. I followed them and saw a half dozen different sized browns hiding around the falls. This wasn't my first encounter with brown trout, but it was my first encounter with so many. The first time I saw a brown trout I was looking for hellbenders in Pisgah National Forest.

I was in a deep pool a hundred yards downstream of a 50 foot waterfall. The creek on the left shoaled to a foot deep where gravel accumulated and steeply sloped to a bedrock-lined six-foot deep pool on the right side of the stream. I enjoyed the crystal clear water and swam against the current, intent on seeing a hellbender. A recently fallen oak tree lay across the entire stream just above the water's surface and one of its thick branches was completely submerged.

My snorkel rubbed against the underside of the tree as I passed. I looked to my left and a two-foot long rotund brown trout stared back at me from his position on a clean bedrock shelf right under the large branch. Its yellow belly glowed against the red bedrock. We watched each other for a few minutes, the trout unsure of what to make of me, until it finally had enough of my presence and rocketed to deeper water. The large butter belly was a total surprise and thrill, even if it is a non-native fish.

The native trout populations in many streams have been replaced by non-native rainbow trout. Rainbows are native to the western US. We raise rainbow trout in hatcheries and release them for fishermen to fish out. The put and take ritual is repeated every spring. Rainbows are the most widely introduced trout globally and putting them in a river changes the energy flow dynamics of the stream to the same degree as removing all of the trees surrounding it.

Brown trout, originally from Europe, are also stocked and have established widespread wild breeding populations. They often replace the native brook trout. I'm pretty certain the browns I saw in Pisgah and Tucquan were breeding wild populations, and while not native, they were exciting to watch.

But nothing is more thrilling than watching native brook trout in cold mountain streams.

Climbers Run is another Susquehanna Riverland stream protected by the Lancaster Conservancy. It looks like it belongs in the mountains of western Pennsylvania more than in the farmlands of Lancaster. Climbers Run tumbles clear and cold over schist shelves through a hemlock lined gorge and the first time I got in I instantly saw a brook trout.

Brook trout are one of our most beautiful native fish. They have red bellies and white-fringed, red pectoral fins, red tails, with orange and yellow spots on a crimson-sided body that grades to dark, tiger striped green above. I watched as the dappled sunlight penetrated the water to make the fish blaze as they hunted food from the swift current. Brook trout require cold, clear water with little sediment. Therefore the streams they inhabit have forested watersheds, which is a rare commodity these days.

A recent EPA report predicts there will be no native trout east of the Mississippi in 90 years, by the year 2100, due to climate change. This is possibly within my children's life time, definitely within my grandkids' lifetime. This frightening prediction should be a loud wakeup call and it makes places like Climbers all the more special. Brook trout in streams like Climbers means we are doing something right to protect the environment. There is great joy in watching native trout in pristine streams.

Rainbow Ballet

I held on to the ledge of a large slab of bedrock, that was like an island surrounded by a sand and gravel bottom and pulled myself over the top in a foot of water. Against a strong sheet flow, I hung upside down over the side of the rock and looked into the dark void beneath. I didn't know what I would find. Maybe a bass. Maybe a trout, maybe a large angry catfish wanting to smash in my mask. It took a minute for my eyes to adjust from bright daylight to dark shadow but when they did, I was dazzled by shimmering red and silver bodies. The 50 strong school of rosy-sided dace kept their heads pointed upstream and moved in unison—a beautiful choreography of red and silver. I watched for a while then left the fish alone, peeled off the rock, and let the current carry me through a shallow riffle, where I bounced from rock to rock until a shimmering rainbow caught my attention off to the side.

Another school of rosy-sided dace danced above a patch of clean gravel nestled between two slabs of schist bedrock. Rainbow squiggles of red, green, and blue darted in circles above the sediment free patch. They looked like a swarm of neon tetras, only four times the size. Rosy-sided dace spawned over nests of other fish, and what looked like two creek chubs hunkered on the bottom. I wondered if their clean gravel nest was the site of this reproductive ballet.

Spring is an amazing time. The world awakens, and just as the great freshwater migrations trickle to an end, the dramatic flashes of breeding fish color take over. All in the streams right in our back yards.

I always like being surprised on snorkeling trips. We form opinions based on how things look from the outside, often without considering what's inside, and when I look inside streams, I'm usually surprised by the beauty, drama, and ecology of even our most familiar and unsuspecting creeks.

Coopers Branch is like that. It's a suburbanized stream, surrounded by houses, roads and shopping centers. It isn't much more than a trickle and it just doesn't look like there should be much to see beneath the surface. I was there to lead a school trip and looked forward to guiding students through their exploration of the little creek. I looked beneath the surface of Coopers Branch while I waited for students to arrive.

Two distinct schools of rosy-sided dace shot from rock to rock and congregated on two different clean gravel patches to spawn. It was an incredible sight for two reasons: rosy-sided dace are some of the most ornately colored fish we have living in our streams, especially when they are spawning, and rosy sides usually need water that's less fouled by sediments. Some fish species can tolerate sedimentation better than others and rosy- sides are one that doesn't do well with muddy water, possibly because they depend primarily on eyesight to find food, and when the water is murky they can't see.

Their presence in suburbanized Coopers Branch indicated that maybe the creek wasn't as impacted as I'd initially thought, based on my observations from the surface. Rosy-sides are still abundant throughout their range—in rocky flowing pools, in headwater creeks, and small rivers from the lower Delaware to the Savanna and Ohio Rivers. However, they have been lost from some streams due to pollution and siltation. It's a great example of why we shouldn't take anything common for granted. Things don't stay common forever. But there was a little rainbow ballet of rosy-sides in that suburbanized creek, and I soaked in every minute of their artistic display.

Invasive Strength and Agility

I could see the large tails of two carp sticking out from under a void beneath a boulder that framed part of the hole. The two fish darted from their hiding spot with one effortless flick of their tails when I swam to the bottom to try to get a better view. I drifted downriver and strained my way back up through the same hole, always just a few feet behind the carp, suckers and chubs on the bottom, and the bluegill and shiners in midwater, who are always able to negotiate the current with ease. Two large carp rocketed out of a deeper pool into my periphery, surprising me, and descended into another hole on the other side of a schist ridge.

Carp are good at startling me. I explored a large pool in the Elk Creek one winter. I drifted over folds of bedrock that reached up from the bottom. There wasn't much life to see since the water was barely above freezing, but still I enjoyed the sensation of flying over wonderful river bottom architecture. My mind was lulled into the here and now as I drifted downstream. A medium-sized carp darted from the protection of one of the bedrock prongs back upstream and scared me more than I scared it. Awfully nimble and fast for a fish that's often characterized as sluggish and fat. I just couldn't respond as agilely or gracefully. All I could do was gasp.

I swam with a school of shad one spring during their migration. The shad scattered as if a large predator had just entered the scene and an eerie stillness fell over the pool. Then it came up through the center of the pool against the current like the shad: a large Asian carp. The two-foot long fish was twice as long and three times as wide as the shad.

Shad spend their lives at sea and move into rivers and streams in spring to spawn. They are built with compact bodies and powerful caudal fins to make such a journey. Carp are more tubular and rotund, better built for lakes and slow moving water than the rapid I snorkeled in. But that carp was able to move against the current with as much grace as the migrants, even though its body type is obviously not well suited for that environment, and I wondered what it was doing there, moving upstream with the sleek lined shad.

There are six species of carp in North America, each one introduced. Asian carp were brought to North America to control algae and aquatic plant growth in aquaculture operations. They escaped captivity and are now considered an invasive species in most freshwater systems. They can alter habitats, which results in the reduction of other species. They are herbivores and effectively out-eat other fish. Billions of dollars are being spent on trying to keep them from entering the Great Lakes, and sometimes I wonder if it's all folly. Once the genie is out of the bottle, it's pretty hard to put it back, especially when the genie is wet and slippery.

They root up submerged vegetation beds as they feed and reproduce where I live on the upper Chesapeake Bay, which destroys habitat for native fish. But still, they are amazing fish to swim with. Most of the fish I encounter when I snorkel are small, one foot or less. The majority are less than six inches long. It's a thrill to swim with two to three foot long fish that weigh ten to twenty pounds, and to experience their strength, agility, and power. Invasive or not.

6. Risks and the Power of Water

Into the Wash

Into The Wash. That's what swimming into a rapid feels like. Like getting tossed into a washing machine. I floated down the lower reach of the Octoraro that contains a few small sets of rapids. Nothing too big or serious, a class two, which are simple enough in a kayak. But it's a different world in the rapid rather than on top of the rapid. Even a simple class two felt a bit treacherous. The bottom came up from four feet to two and the pace quickened. What had been easy to swim against was now impossible. The only way to stop was to grab on to a rock.

The water sped up and spilled through a *V* between two boulders, and I was in the middle of it. There was no stopping. Even grabbing on to a rock wasn't an option without risking a dislocated shoulder. The best I could do was fend off fast approaching boulders before I plowed into them. I was poured over rocks and squeezed between them, just like the water that carried me. And while this rapid was fairly benign by kayaking standards, it had the potential to be more dangerous to snorkelers. One unprotected move and I could go head first into a boulder. A different wrong move and my chest could impact. Brain and lungs could be involved. I felt my heart quicken when I realized the danger. Fight or flight kicked in, and I couldn't run so I was in for the fight.

I'm not one to work against rivers, but rather with them. I'm not big on me vs. them when it comes to nature. I think that's a pretty human-centered, simplistic view. But the rapid sure felt like we were opponents, when in fact the river could have cared less about my outcome. It did what it did: send water downstream, over, through, and around rocks, whether I was there or not. I was just another very large leaf that was either going to float out the end of the rapid, or get hung up somewhere in the middle. I kept my arms up to fend off rocks. It was a wax on, wax off kind of thing.

The rush of the water was deafeningly loud, like being in a 60 mile per hour wind. And still there was life there. A darter hunkered down in a gap between rocks and an eel emerged from under another one. The water tried to pull my mask from my face and it tried to twist my snorkel from its band. It was hard to breathe due to the force of the water pushing against my chest.

The rapid was a chaos of bubbles and I had to rely on the flow of water to determine direction a few times. I finally reached the bottom of the rapid, spent. My arms and legs were rubber, and my abdominal muscles were tight. Down river lay a stretch of calm water below a loud, frenzied rapid.

Creek snorkeling is what you make it, and what you want it to be. It can be a relaxing silent float, an awe inspiring exploration, or an adrenaline-pumping, somewhat dangerous downstream ride. Snorkeling through that rapid gave me a different perspective, a new rush, and I will swim rapids again.

Part of the draw of creek and river snorkeling is witnessing the brilliance of freshwater life. Part of it is exploring areas most haven't seen underwater, and part of it is experiencing creeks and rivers on their terms, like swimming through rapids. On another trip, I snorkeled the last few miles of Susquehanna more to experience the Susquehanna on its terms than to witness riverine ecology in action, and that made me a little nervous.

The water was murky and cold and if things went just a little wrong, I could find myself in a lot of trouble. I was going to snorkel a three mile section of the Susquehanna from Octoraro Creek to just north of Port Deposit. This isn't a particularly dangerous part of river. There aren't any killer rapids, but a lot of people have died here. It was cold, so if one thing went wrong that caused me to be on the river for longer than planned, or if my drysuit failed for any reason, I was at real risk of becoming hypothermic. Then there were the usual drowning hazards.

I was familiar with my chosen section of river, which heightened my caution. It was controlled by the Conowingo Dam, or as controlled as we fool ourselves that dams control. Ultimately the river does what it wants, when it wants, and each spring the lower Susquehanna reminds us all of that fact when she floods, in spite of Conowingo. But today the dam dictated the river, so water levels changed drastically in an instant.

The risks I mentally listed included strainers and rocks. I wanted to make sure to swim clear of the heads of islands, rocks, and anything else that might catch and hold logs in the water that strain the water through them, but capture larger objects, like me. Strainers are usually fatal. One wrong rocky snag on my drysuit and I'd be exposed to 39 degree water and 29 degree air. Access to that stretch of river was limited so while I don't consider it remote, rescue is difficult. If something went wrong, I was on my own. River snorkeling is largely a safe activity, but extra caution was warranted in this case.

The river was flowing at 10,000 cubic feet per second; gauge height was at 11 feet when I left my truck at the take out, and I figured one of the problems I might face was the shallow nature of the river. If I had to repeatedly walk, my time in the water would be longer than what I wanted, given the cold.

The Susquehanna's rocky snaggle-toothed character was evident through the low water. By the time I was dropped off at the put in three miles upstream, the dam was flowing 50,000 cubic feet per second, the river rose three feet, and my worry was now too much water moving so fast that it could drive me into a strainer or exposed rock. I wouldn't have much control relative to the force of the river.

I flowed out from the Octoraro and hoped the visibility would improve once I was clear of its muddy trail. . Finally, the bottom came into view and blurred past as I approached the head of a gravel bar submerged by the rising flow. I swam toward the middle of the river, and floated with the current. An immature eagle circled close overhead and seemed curious about what I was. A mature eagle took flight from a shoreline tree when I was next to it and multiple herons grunted off rocks as I passed.

Unseen rock behemoths forced large mushroom waves of water up from the bottom. Leaves that fell and entered the river during the autumn were churned up with other bits of detritus, swirling, becoming pulverized. This is the food that drives much of the river ecosystem, and every time I approached a place where the water was forced up, I witnessed the process of detritus cycling that is so critical to the river's ecology. But mostly I felt the river's raw power. It pushed me past rock outcrops, and pulled me back into eddies. It threw my feet to the surface when I floated over upwelling mushrooms. Its strength coursed through me.

Occasionally, large rocks emerged through the murk then disappeared just as fast, but for the most part, I only felt their effects. I learned that splashing on the horizon meant the approach of a rapid, so I occasionally lifted my face from the water to scan downstream. I wanted to spend more time in the rapids, to play in the eddies, but didn't want to take more risks. I wasn't sure exactly how long the trip would take, and my hands were already painfully numb. I wanted to hang behind some of the larger rocks to see if any fish were holding. I wanted to investigate some of the small tributary streams that flowed into the Susquehanna. But most of all I wanted to make it, so I passed up the urge to explore and kept heading downstream.

I reached the take out without incident, a lot faster than I'd expected, and good thing. My hands were so numb they were almost useless. I was barely able to open my truck door and start it for some heat. The rewarming process was excruciating.

That trip gave me a completely new perspective on the river, a new and different understanding and respect. I felt proud that I'd faced the fear of being alone on big water without a boat. Mostly it made me want to come back to explore some more with mask and snorkel. There's so much river and so little time.

Water is powerful whether it flows in a large river or small stream. The Principio isn't big, about ten feet across, but the water there is just as powerful as the water I experienced on the Susquehanna. I clawed along the bottom of the Principio Creek to pull my way upstream in two feet of smooth but quickly flowing water. When I let go of a stone or boulder, I was swept downriver until I was able to dig my toes into the cobbles. I drifted into an eddy slowed by the root-filled shoreline and came nose to nose with a tessellated darter who had excavated a home from the sand underneath a small cobble, well out of the flow. I swam back toward the middle of the river and allowed the current to carry me downstream. I peeked above the surface every few minutes to gauge how far I had before the river shallowed. It would take some time and effort to stop short of the boulders that formed a downstream set of rapids.

I cautiously entered the short rapid and held on to a boulder with one hand, which allowed my body to trail behind in the strong current. Ameletid mayfly nymphs clung to the lee side of rocks. Their black and white-banded frilly tails waved in the turbulent water. The darter and mayflies have all devised graceful ways to brace themselves against the flow that I clumsily struggled against.

The bedrock below was scoured smooth, and a submerged whirlpool twirled a stone in a circle that wore a small cup in the rock. Water shaped the course of the river and set its depth. It placed, moved, and restructured the rocks that formed the rapid. Water is a dynamic force. It's never finished working and the river shifted and changed before my eyes. It would be a different place the next day, and almost unrecognizable the next year. The holes I'd known six months prior were either deeper or gone. One rapid was now a short falls. Nothing is static.

I see water restructure rivers regularly, but especially after rains. Recently, an inch and a half of rain raised the level of Basin Run by four feet and turned it to chocolate milk. Three days later the water wasn't as murky and the water level dropped but the flow was still greater than what I'd been used to at that spot.

The water was hazy but clear enough to see the bottom. I hung on to the edges of boulders as I crossed the rapid to the far shore, feeling like a leaf in a hurricane. Sand gathered in large mounds in the lee of shoreline rock, and a few minnows lazily drifted from their protective eddies. The high velocity water rearranged the parts of the bottom it could and tornados of sand and rock swirled in eddies behind boulders. The water uprooted some Asian clams from the bottom and piled them with a mound of pebbles behind a rock. Part of the bank was cut deeper, exposing more tree roots.

I watched the river shape itself as I clawed upstream. There is a feeling of permanence that comes with watching a river. Rain falls, rivers rise, water wears away rock. That stream was there long before me, and it would be there long after I am gone. In the mean time I would enjoy some moments in its current and I felt completely free as I drifted downstream through the rapid, entirely at the mercy of the water. It's reassuring and life-affirming to know that there are things much larger than I at work in the world, and I get to play a small role. One of those immortal processes is the erosion of rock by water.

Water wears away rock. It seems this is a universal truth. Roman philosopher Lucretius noticed the process when he wrote "The fall of dripping water wears away the stone." A Chinese proverb observed the power of persistent water: "Water dropping day by day wears the hardest rock away." And Job makes the same proclamation in the Bible: "The waters wear the stones." The pot rocks on the Gunpowder River, so named for the pot holes carved into the schist bedrock by eons of water, is an example of this phenomena. Maybe that's the draw of that place. We can see tangible evidence that persistence does produce results. Water does wear away rock, given enough time.

The smoothed rock felt warm as I suited up, and its mica flecked blue and white bands were striking. The area brought back memories of a favorite family vacation to Ausable Chasm in New York. My parents weren't great outdoors people. Neither one had an outdoor background, but that didn't stop them from taking us on incredible adventures. We all learned how to camp at the same time. I think about these formative journeys much more since my parents died, and it's a rare day in a river when I don't think of them at least once.

One of those adventures was to Ausable Chasm. Ausable Chasm is a river-carved canyon where the Ausable River cuts through the geology of the Adirondacks. It's a vertical sided gorge, labeled the "Grand Canyon of the Adirondacks." The trails are narrow and carved into the chasm walls, and they lead past water-carved potholes. I spent a week exploring Ausable and the surrounding rivers, fishing and snorkeling the clear Adirondack streams with my parents when I was eight. The Ausable potholes are on a much more grand scale, in a much more dramatic canyon. But the pot rocks on the Gunpowder do a fine job proving that water in fact does wear away rock.

I slipped into a slow-moving section of river, partly protected from the main flow by a wall of jagged bedrock, and I scrambled upstream. It was hard to hold on to smooth and slick schist. The flow intensified as I approached a short falls, and the water became turbulent with disorienting air bubbles. I dived for the bottom a few feet below and scrambled to find any lip to hold on to. The rock was worn smooth and sticks were wedged into a crack between two slabs.

I let go and let the current carry me downstream where I crossed a gravel bar and entered the main flow of the Gunpowder. It wasn't an especially large or powerful river, but all of its energy seemed to be focused where water from the piedmont quickly falls to meet the coastal plain.

I thought I saw a ghost school of shad waiting in the large eddy below the forceful rapid, but second-guessed myself as it was the wrong time of year to have shad there. I tried to stand in the five-foot deep water but the force of what appeared to be a gentle upstream eddy swept me off my feet and tried to push me into the main fast, hard flow. I swam against the eddy, downstream, and confirmed they weren't ghosts. The school of a dozen shad zipped into the gloom.

The power of the water was intense and the large eddy continued to try to swirl me into the main flow. I was in a remote spot, yet I felt watched. I felt reluctant and nervous. Scared even. I felt like nothing more than a leaf swirled around in the drift. I felt insignificant. Just another speck in the river. I had minimal control on where I go. I was at the mercy of the river, and felt humbled and grounded.

And maybe that grounding is part of the attraction to the truth: that water wears rock. It reminds us that everything, even things that seem infinitely permanent and unmovable like rock (or my parents, as I thought of them), are ephemeral. The sooner we accept this, the sweeter life becomes. Rivers are great teachers of this lesson.

Night

It was a few weeks before Thanksgiving and I needed to get into the water. Shorter days and longer nights meant I needed to snorkel in the dark, which was fine. Except that I don't like the dark very much. But still, I like snorkeling more than I dislike the dark, so I decided to take advantage of the first full moon after Halloween to get into the river; mostly just to get in, but also to experience that other worldly realm.

Terrestrial systems are different at night. They look different; they feel different. There are different creatures out. Things act differently. But still they are familiar. I expected the night time Octoraro to be completely foreign. The place I have visited underwater hundreds of times would be, I was sure, hard to recognize.

I got to the water's edge and frequently looked over my shoulder. I was thankful for the full moon that lit up the stream valley with a warm blue hue. But I wouldn't have called it welcoming. There's a lot of human history there, and I've experienced a lot of tragedy in that area. I've responded to drownings, overdoses, fatal car accidents, and shootings, all within a mile of that spot, and their ghosts seemed close. So while the guiding moonlight took the edge off my nervousness, I was still a little jumpy.

I zipped up my drysuit, wriggled into my hood, and slid on my mask. I stepped into the stream, lay down and was instantly disoriented. The spot I'd visited thousands of times was so different in the dark, where I could only see whatever was illuminated in a small foot-wide circle of light. Familiar boulder, log, and root landmarks were hidden.

An eel rocketed upstream out of my beam of light. They were supposed to be migrating right about then, on a moonless night near Halloween, so I figured I'd missed them by a week. Or maybe the mythical mass migration was just a ghost too; a figment of what once was. I've never seen it, and I'm pretty sure that eel was a young one who was just out hunting.

Algae covered the bottom and waved in the current like fine black hair. Leaves in the drift came into view just before they struck my mask, which made me more nervous. There didn't seem to be any fish, but I thought that either I was looking in the wrong places, or they'd taken off as soon as my light touched them. The bottom was a monotonous expanse of sand and gravel, in a stretch of stream that should have been riffle.

Erosion puts more sand and gravel into streams and covers the nooks and crannies of a diverse habitat like rock and cobble, which cuts down on the number of species and individuals present. It looked like a hairy desert at night, and the algal fur comes from too much nitrogen that we unintentionally put into water by driving too much, not maintaining our septics, and over-fertilizing our lawns.

Rocks came into view only after I was right upon them, it seemed, even though my beam extended ten feet upstream. A small school of minnows hung and fed in the eddy. Finally, some life besides algae. Even though they were a nondescript muddy brown, their metallic sides glistened when my flashlight caught them just right. Always there is hidden beauty. Vision confined to a light beam became normal, and I started to head upstream into the current. I hoped to see more nocturnal life, to observe the nighttime workings of familiar daytime ecology. Just as I got used to the unsettling feeling of leaves striking my mask without warning, and restricted vision, my light quit. I was in the middle of the stream with no light, and leaves plastered to my mask by the current. Time to leave. I drifted toward the bank where I'd started and hauled out of the stream.

Moonlight reflected like white paint swirled on a black sea as I peeled off my wetsuit hood and drysuit. I felt more at ease. The only real ghosts there were the ones I'd concocted, and the ones of clean and abundant streams past.

Nighttime snorkeling has become a regular activity for me in winter when days are too short to allow for daylight trips after work. Basin Run glistened as the last bit of winter's orange light evaporated from the western sky. I slipped the dive headlamp over my wetsuit hood. The light perched on top of my mask in a perfect spot to see who might be out on a cold winter's night. The water looked clear from the surface, and during the day it would be, but the headlamp light reflects back from each of the tiniest of particles in the water and the beam shines through a faint haze. The water looks like someone added a few drops of milk to a clean pitcher of water.

There wasn't much to see initially. The view was very different due to the different lighting. Stands of rockweed looked like deep sea black corals in the spotlight of a submersible. A single fish stuck its head from behind a rock. Some kind of minnow, a kind I hadn't seen there during the day. I explored the deeper crevasses hoping to see some more fish life, hoping to learn the nighttime ecology, but only see more deep sea coral-like rockweed, and a single snail. I had just been there in daylight and had found an incredible abundance and diversity of fish, but there wasn't much out at night. Where had they gone? Do different species emerge at night? Who are the nocturnal players in that stream?

I headed back downstream with more questions than answers, but that's also part of the beauty of snorkeling streams: constant discovery and exploration.

A few months later, I returned after the same stream iced over. A pool of open water extended 15 feet downstream at the base of a small riffle. Beyond that, a solid sheet of ice encased the stream. Getting swept downstream that night would be fatal. My headlamp reflected off the white snow on the ice but the light was eaten by the dark water.

I suited up on the snow-covered shore and fumbled in the dark to find gear in my bag: hood, gloves, mask, and camera. I slid down the bank and was a little worried about scrambling over the ice-covered boulders that made up that part of Basin Run's shoreline to get into the water. I didn't expect to see much life. I was going in mostly to experience the accumulation of anchor ice, the flocculent bits that form and cluster in the lee of boulders. I was going to admire the nocturnal winter sculpture of the river. The air was 20 degrees, -10 degrees with wind chill, and the water was a degree above freezing. It would have to be a quick trip—a fast aquatic fix to get me through the next few frigid days, until temperatures climbed above freezing again.

I braced for the usual painful, cold shock, but it didn't happen. The barely above-freezing water felt warm compared to the air. Something shot out from under me into the current, and swam around me. It looked like a large leech. I've seen those in freezing water before; then it looked more like an eel. Finally, I was able to make a positive identification: it was a lamprey. This ancient jawless fish looked clean and silver, free from blemish. Very different than the last lamprey I'd seen, beaten at the end of its life's journey. Lamprey migrate into streams to spawn. The lamprey I'd seen two Mays ago had been at the end of its run. The juvenile on that snorkel was just starting, and it looked young—new and shiny.

The lamprey and I swam together, but mostly the lamprey tried to escape my flashlight beam. The current pushed me into an anchor ice shelf and the lamprey swam under it. I kept watching as the lamprey searched for a hiding spot a few feet away. I was tempted to follow the fish under the ice shelf, but there was only one way out: the way in and that would be against the current. I decided to watch the lamprey from a few feet away and hoped I had a good enough shot. Sometimes I forget that it's more about being there experiencing the underwater river than it is about documenting it.

The lamprey successfully wriggled out of sight and I resumed my initial mission to explore the accumulation of flocculent ice. It was easy to fool myself that I was exploring some arctic creek as my light glowed through the underside of the ice that extended behind larger rocks in the river. I could see the masses grow as buoyant inch-long frozen bits float downstream and stick to their comrades.

The cold finally took its toll and I needed to get out. My feet froze to the snow-covered ground and stuck with each step as I moved toward my gear bag and safety light set up a little further up the bank. My flashlight froze and I quickly wiped off my camera before the water iced up. My drysuit got stiff and crinkly. My chin stuck when it touched the ice on the suit. The moon started to rise and lightened the dark night. It was an amazing trip. I witnessed two, eons old phenomena: lamprey that predate bony fish and other vertebrates in the fossil record, and the process of freezing water in a moving river. What an amazing world we live in.

Winter isn't the only time to witness the nocturnal workings of our rivers and I am making more attempts to get into the rivers at night in warmer months. I explored the nocturnal Delaware on a recent spring time trip. Shad spawn nocturnally, so I hoped to witness that event. I was almost positive I was camped in the same site my dad and I had camped in 40 years ago. He's been dead for 15 years, and I still feel his absence. But that trip to the Delaware so long ago still stands out vividly in my memory. My dad didn't know it at the time but he was instilling a deep love of rivers in me.

Shad splashed all night. It was cold, dropping to 35 degrees, and I really wasn't prepared for the frigid air temperatures, so as tempted as I was to get up at two a.m. and snorkel to witness the nocturnal shad spawn, I didn't. I banked on the shad spawning again the next night when the air was forecast to be 20 degrees warmer.

So I waited on the shores of the Delaware in the same spot my dad and I had stood in so long ago, and reminisced while the sun finally slipped below the horizon. I waited to hear the shad tails slap the surface. Returning always makes me a little sad, and brings up memories of a past that can't be recovered, one where I didn't know what I had until it was gone. But I was there in that moment, and the shad finally started to move. I geared up and got in. I'm not wasting any time any more.

The Delaware, like any river, is such a different world at night. The water was clean and the light shone through the water onto the dark bottom. Beds of mussels were open and filtering, their reddish tan flesh apparent between the partly opened dark shells. Aquatic plants looked brilliant green in my light as they sprouted from the bottom. Smaller eels and elvers, juvenile eels, were abundant and hunted around and under rocks. White webby strands drifted downriver along the bottom and I wondered what they were. Then I realized that they were probably mussel glochidia. Mussels produce glochidia that need fish in order to survive. Glochidia are juvenile mussels that need to transform into adults. They need fish to complete their metamorphosis. Kind of like caterpillars turning into butterflies, only glochidia look more like small mussels not caterpillars. They live parasitically on fish for about a month then drop to the river bottom and become adults. Eastern elliptios, the most abundant mussel there, depend on American eels for their glochidia to latch to, so they produce them in web-like strands that stick to the eels as they slime through the substrate. Ingenious system. I felt fortunate to be able to witness their release.

The shad looked like mirrored, silver slabs and darted out of darkness, into the halo of light for an instant then disappeared. While they were too fast for me to capture on film, I watched their spawning rituals as males chased females in tight circles. Night snorkeling always gives me a new perspective on places I visit regularly. There's a whole new ecology revealed by the darkness.

But as amazing as nocturnal snorkeling is, it still takes me a little time to get used to being underwater at night. I don't know why but I successfully freaked myself out on one particular trip to Basin Run. Thoughts of a body we pulled out of the creek ten years prior dominated my mind. I have nocturnally snorkeled there at least a dozen times, and not once did I focus on the night we recovered the body. But that night, for some reason, visions of the young man lying in the creek bed set up shop and were reluctant to leave. It made me want to continually look over my shoulder.

I got into the water that was still cold with winter, and my existence tightened into the tiniest circle of light. The world became whatever my headlamp lit. Everything else was black. I started to feel claustrophobic. I picked my head up out of the water and could barely make out the opposite shore, even though it was only ten feet away. The creek felt so big from the surface, but underwater it felt like I was swimming in a linen closet. I could only see what felt like a dime sized spot of light. I was on a very alien world, as if I'd left Earth and landed underwater on some foreign planet full of ghosts. And I'd thought I knew the place.

A large case-maker caddis fly hunkered in the sand behind a larger rock. Some kind of minnow stayed motionless in the lee of another. I forgot about the ghost of the man we'd pulled out. I forgot about the aliens. The fish didn't move, but tolerated my closeness, headlamp spotlight and blinding flash as I snapped pictures. I didn't know what kind of fish they were, but that didn't matter. My world came into focus on that fish. It was just me and the fish and that moment. Which is one of the draws of river snorkeling and exploration. It puts me into the now. It grounds me. River snorkeling, day or night, refocuses my attention on what is real and important and it makes the aliens and ghosts disappear.

Screaming Barfies

I'd just gotten out of the Brandywine at the Natural Lands Trust Stroud Preserve after a short, but cold, snorkel and my hands were in excruciating pain. The water was barely above freezing and the air was below. A biting wind blew down the length of the river, and I expected the overcast sky to drop snow or sleet any minute. We'd been overdue for a bit of cold weather.

I turned and let the gentle current carry me downstream under the small arch bridge. The pace quickened since the water shallowed and the bottom got more interesting as it became rocky with more holes and places for fish to hide. A large chub darted along the bottom of one of the deeper pools with one flick of its tail. A second one followed and I tried to chase them to get a decent picture, but they easily outswam me. Beds of submerged vegetation poked from the sandy parts of the bottom like beard stubble. A belted kingfisher tried to figure me out as I floated toward a sand bar where I could walk out of the river back toward my truck, and hoped that my hands would work enough for me to unzip my dry suit. I couldn't feel them, after just 30 minutes.

Screaming barfies is a term used in ice climbing to describe when hands and fingers get so cold they hurt to the point of nausea when they rewarm, and that phrase applied to my hands after that trip. Ice formed on my dry suit as I peeled out of it. My hands didn't work very well. I felt nauseous as they warmed up; the sharp pain was intense.

Was it worth it? Absolutely. I'd seen large chubs, submerged vegetation below the surface, and belted kingfishers above. Snorkeling freshwater systems gives a real sense of exploration. Even though the river had been visited by thousands if not hundreds of thousands of people, I could be fairly certain no one else had snorkeled here. And I was even more certain that no one had snorkeled there in winter. It felt like going where no one else had gone, seeing things most people missed. The Brandywine is an amazing place in the middle of winter, as are most of our rivers. They are usually not snorkeled in summer and ignored in winter so the sense and feel of being an explorer is real. The chance to learn something that would be new to science about winter river ecology is huge.

So I head to our rivers year round, driven by a desire to discover, by a need for adventure, and to watch how life responds as the fall winds down and temperatures drop. Fish get lethargic, and then disappear. Riffles that were chock full of fish become barren and soon trips are more for experiencing the architecture of the stream than they are for watching the drama of aquatic survival. Every winter I chase life till it mysteriously disappears. I want to know where the fish go when it gets cold, and each fall I try to learn the wintertime fate of another species. I look forward to the November when I discover where all the other species go.

I went to the Brandywine one early winter day. The water was invitingly clear. It was going to be a good trip regardless of whether I saw shiners or trout or darters or any other life. Stream structure and geology can be just as intriguing. I waded into knee deep water and lay down over a sandy bottom. It was difficult to hold against the strong current without any rocks to grab. Drifts of sand played across the bottom as mica flecks sparkled. Small scalloped dunes formed and washed away with each flow change in that temporary place.

I crawled upstream on fingertips and toes and headed toward the cobbled middle. Brilliant green algae with strands of red covered the rocks and stood at attention downstream. Orange yellow quartz boulders were scoured clean of any growth on their upstream sides, and perfectly round, smooth caddis fly cases were glued fast.

I enjoyed trying to solve the puzzle of the Brandywine's geologic past. I admired how water shaped rock and rock affected water, and how the hydroscape reflected all of these eons-old forces to produce a view that lasts for just one moment in time and then is forever changed.

I noticed a cylindrical tube of fish hunkered down in the gravel, between two pieces of mica, which drew my attention to the spot. I would have never seen the northern hog sucker if it hadn't been for the glint of mica. Northern hog suckers are one of those fish whose wintertime whereabouts puzzled me. Is that where they go for the winter? Were they always present, but were just so well camouflaged that I couldn't detect their presence unless I was literally on top of them? Their motion gave them away when it was warmer and they were more active. They usually shot off before I could decipher them from their background due to their cryptic coloration. But the one I'd spotted stayed put, probably because of the cold and I was able to appreciate its gold tipped fins and green banded body.

The force of the water was still tremendous in the center of the stream so I struggled upstream and toward river left, where a nice eddy swirled behind a finger of gravel that protruded into the river. As I crawled along I found two spiny, checked crayfish mating in the gravel. More life and the drama of its procreation on the cusp of the winter, when life slowed, hid, seemed to just hang on. But maybe that's just my perception based on not seeing life out and about flaunting its existence the way it does in our summertime streams. Maybe life is always there and abundant. We just need to look in the right way to see it, from the right perspective.

I floated into the eddy and rested. Movement caught my attention. A school of common shiners with brilliant peach pectoral and anal fins fed in the drift. The fish held against the current, then drifted downstream, shot into the eddy and repeated in a swirling calculated pattern of hunting for prey I couldn't see. They were intent on feeding so my presence was hardly noticed, except that they enjoyed devouring the stuff I inadvertently kicked into the water column as I clawed upstream.

The cold water started to chill through my dry suit and fleece layer. My mouth was getting numb and hands were hard to move. It was time to leave. I let go of the rock that kept me stationary on the edge of the eddy and floated in the lifeless flow. There was plenty of life there below me between the rocks and cobble that I couldn't see, just nothing obvious in the water column.

This was the beginning of the wintertime transformation of the Brandywine, the changing of the biological cast that is obvious in our rivers, which have a seasonal progression of life that is hidden from common knowledge, mostly because we don't look. Thick algae covers the bottoms of streams right around leaf fall in autumn, and the caddisflies come out in force in the winter. Mayflies alternate with the caddis through the cold months. Migrants like shad and herring follow the caddis in spring, and minnows become abundant through the summer.

There is a rapid in Deer Creek that goes through a seasonal transition of bottom dwelling insects. May flies give way to caddis as the water chills and in January it's the case-maker caddisflies turn to rule this rapid. I see that hundreds cover rocks and cling to pieces of rockweed all pointed upstream to keep oxygenated water flowing through their cases as I got into Deer Creek on a mid-winter day. They extended two legs up into the current to snag morsels of food on their stiff hairs.

The first skim ice had formed and the water hurt my lips, chin, and lower cheeks—the only skin I have exposed—and felt like thousands of weak jellyfish stings. Rosy-sided and black-nosed dace were sluggish in the cold water compared to their energetic motions of a month ago. I always wondered what these fish did in winter. Some of the studies I've read indicated they headed for deeper water, and I hadn't seen them on my last few trips, since about Thanksgiving. So I figured they did what the studies said and headed downriver for deeper water. I'd missed their presence and was glad to see them again.

Fish are ectotherms. They typically take on the temperature of the surrounding water rather than maintain their own body temperature, which is metabolically costly. Look at how many calories we endotherms need to consume daily to maintain our 98.6 degree furnace. Some fish even have glyco proteins and glyco lipids, basically antifreeze molecules, in their blood that give them the ability to survive freezing temperatures. And some fish, like the tuna, can actually maintain a body temperature that is warmer than the surrounding water. But the fish in our streams take on the temperature of the surrounding water, and things tend to slow down in the cold—except for the pace of the water flow.

I thought the fish would have headed downstream to deeper water earlier, as all the field guides say, but maybe they would stay in the deeper pools of the creek through the winter. As much as I have snorkeled that pool in that stream, each time something different is revealed. The creek changes minute by minute, fish by fish, flow by flow, season by season, year to year. It's never the same.

A few weeks later I got into Big Branch. What I thought was skim ice was a bit thicker and it took almost all of my weight to break it into large chunks so that I could make it to the main part of Big Branch.

The water ran clear and freezing cold. I slipped into Big Branch as soon as I cleared the ice chunks. The frigid water stung my lips and my teeth started to hurt from the cold. The water was about as clear as I'd ever seen it, and I started a slow crawl upstream. The river had been rearranged again by heavy summer flows and the large downstream hole was gone. Beavers were starting to dam the river there and the main channel had been split in two.

I belly hurdled over the first log that was now embedded in the bottom and floated upstream. There had been two deep holes there, but now the depth was more uniform and I realized I was swimming in a newly formed beaver pond. Evidence of the aquatic mammals was abundant and the light greenish white bark stripped chews were piled on the bottom near the bank.

Schools of tiny fish huddled in the lee of logs and looked like small clouds. A large school of common shiner hovered over the bottom like a fog. The fish stayed together as one mass and they slowly moved away from me at first, but then came toward me once they got used to my presence. I noticed there were a few fall fish and a rosy-sided dace or two mixed in.

I headed into the big pool that was framed by a new beaver dam on the downstream side. The bottom 12 feet below was normally out of sight, or just barely visible most of the time. But on that trip it felt like there was nothing between me and the leaves, logs, and stumps below.

Snowstorms not only change landscapes from common place to wondrous, they also transform river snorkeling experiences. I'd waded through snow deeper than the water I was about to snorkel. We'd received two back to back monumental snowstorms and the waist deep drifts I'd struggled through were a testament to the record setting snowfall. One weather event, one season of weather events, even a few years of weather events, isn't enough to say anything about climate. But it's getting harder to define normal around here.

The last time I'd snorkeled that section of Deer Creek, it had been 85 degrees and I'd struggled to find a parking spot among the cars lining the dirt road that runs along this favorite swimming hole. On this day, I struggled to find parking because of ten foot tall snow piles. Deer Creek ran hard and a little high. I knelt in the lee of a grass tuft island near the shore, lay flat, and let the cold water sting my face. The calm near the shore created an expansive plane of coarse pink sand that was scalloped by the current into dunes. I felt like I was flying over the Sahara as I moved toward the center of the channel and the full force of Deer Creek.

My snorkel hummed in the force of the current. I hung on to a large rock with one hand and imagined this is what a kite must feel like in a stiff breeze, until the hundred pound boulder started to lift from the bottom. Snails hunkered down in the branches of an aquatic moss on the lee side of a large rock. An ameletid mayfly swam to the bottom in front of me with its long frilly tails waving in the current and abdominal gills beating the water.

While many mayflies clasp tightly to rocks, this one swims around as it functions as a collector-gatherer. The sand grain homes of Northern case-maker caddisflies lined up like round town homes just under the top edge of a boulder in the middle of the current. Caddis fly cases all essentially serve the same ingenious function: protect the insect larvae inside. But the diversity of form that function takes on is impressive. Blacklegged long-horned case-maker caddis fly larvae crawled about in their coarse tan sand grain homes, while the cases of smooth concentric rings of vegetation constructed by humpless case-maker caddisflies, and the black coarse grained cases of uenoid case-makers, tightly held in the nooks and crannies of large rocks. They all serve the same function, yet their forms are beautifully different. And each one endured the heavy flow and cold water after an historic Mid-Atlantic snow fall.

Snow also transforms the night and snorkeling a familiar stream at night while surrounded by a snow covered landscape gives an even more foreign experience. Even the common when viewed from a different perspective, under different conditions, provides new scenes and excitement that comes from new observations.

A half-moon provided enough ambient light to make the short hike through the fresh snow to the water's edge without a headlamp. The river was up and the water boiled around rocks and under ice sheets. The edge of the river was noticeable in the moonlight as a distinct line where the snow ended and the dark began. I geared up in the dark, and wasn't used to the extra equipment needed for night exploration. I fumbled with the hand light, headlight, and shore light a little.

The water felt huge. This was a familiar hole, but it was unrecognizable when I could only see the little bit revealed in the narrow flashlight beam. The cold water didn't register over the anticipation of being there on a late fall snowy night. I searched for life but didn't see any. I have learned that there is always life present, it's more a question of whether I can spot it or not.

I started to see accreted pebble caddis fly cases attached to rocks. I worked upstream into the next pool and scanned it with my light, hoping to see a fish, but was happy for the experience regardless. The cold was starting to tingle my exposed lips and face. Finally I saw a fish motionless on the bottom with its eye peering over a bedrock ledge. It was a trout. Maybe the same one that had taunted me all year. Every time I slipped into the pool a trout took off before I could even get my camera close to ready for a shot.

Tonight the fish was motionless on the bottom and gave plenty of photographic opportunity. The strobe filled the pool with light and blinded everything in it. I put my other hand down on the bottom to stabilize myself in the current as I crept in for a closer view and something alive shot out from under it. I could feel the power of whatever it was through my wetsuit glove and figured it was another trout.

I took my last shot of the trout and explored the rest of pool in the swift current a bit more. A large tail stuck out from behind a large rock. I peeked over the side and sure enough, there was a good sized northern hog sucker. I tend to see these fish in cold weather and wonder if they are one of the fish that stay active in Basin Run throughout the whole winter.

I looked under the ice sheet that extended out from shore. The ice was clear and took on an aqua hue. Entrained air bubbles looked silver and a red oak leaf was pinned to the underside. This was such a different world, such a different view. My breath was taken away by the beauty rather than the cold.

As winter progresses, ice and snow intensifies and fish become less apparent, but views like that one and the winter river scape keep my attention. Rivers in the Mid-Atlantic freeze near the middle of winter and there is a sequence to it: slush ice forms as water gets colder until finally slush ice chunks form, congregate, and start to flow downstream. Sometimes it builds from the bottom as ice sheets cover the top. It all combines to give an arctic look to common streams.

Deer Creek looked arctic as I approached. I'd recently saw a picture of the Hofsa River in Iceland and it instantly made my bucket list of places to snorkel. Deer Creek reminded me a little of that picture. The water ran clear had taken on an aquamarine hue over the last few days. What I found under the surface was a very different scene. Waves of temperature distortion and flocculent ice suspended throughout the water column significantly reduced visibility. I could still see bottom, but not with the crispness I'd expected. It felt like I was swimming through a partially melted slushy. It was noisy underwater as ice clinked while it flowed downstream and sounded like a muted wind chime. Water lapped at the underside of the ice sheet.

An ice chunk almost ripped my mask off the instant I pulled into faster moving water and ice constantly ground on my mask and hood as it slid past. Ice chunks bounced of my mask as they hurtled downstream.

A tongue of ice formed in the lee of a large rock out in the rapid. I assumed it was just a sheet and I'd be able to peer under it. The water behind the rock provided a refuge from the chaos of the rapid. Sculpin lay their eggs on the downstream face in spring, shad use the lee to climb the rapid in April, caddis flies lay their eggs on it in late summer, and eels hunt around it year round. I looked forward to a view beneath the ice, of the eddy and a rock I've come to know very well over the last five years. What I found was a solid accumulation of slush to the bottom two feet below. Bands of slush filled in some of the gaps on the bottom out in the main flow, looked like coagulated fat, and made everything blurry.

This is a phenomenon called anchor ice that forms during periods of extreme cold. Water dips below the freezing point but ice won't grow on the surface due to the moving water. Ice platelets form in the water column and gather on the bottom. Sometimes anchor ice forms a thick blanket on the bottom of rivers and can cause them to flood. The clear, aquamarine, arctic view I'd enjoyed from the bank was water flowing over anchor ice, not crystal clear water flowing over river bottom.

A dace hovered in the narrow inch wide gap between the ice and the bottom. Pebbles that were plucked off the bottom by the foot thick anchor ice slab were now entrained in the flow that crept downstream. Caddisflies were ground off their rock perches by ice as it moved past. Ice is a huge, shaping force in rivers, even in temperate zones, and when I snorkel a river at this time of year I get a more complete understanding of those interactions. I gain a more thorough appreciation of what life in our rivers and streams experiences throughout the entire year, not just the warmer biologically active parts. And I get to see some absolutely incredible river and ice scapes.

The ice leaves as temperatures climb to just above freezing and the February world assumes the dull gray of monotony. There's about a month to go till things start to come alive again. Not that things are really dead. Life is there, it's just not as active and noticeable. It's nuzzled down into the cobbles instead of flying over the bottom.

The sun sat low in the sky and long shadows were cast early. The stream valley darkened by four. Cold knife points of frigid water stabbed my face and hands as I crawled upstream.

Caddis fly larvae have sealed the openings of their cases with quartz grains as they usually do at about that time. Other caddis were still out grazing. A Northern case-maker caddis fly was clawing at a smooth cobble, as it tried to get a firm grip to hold against the current. A blast of water blew the caddis fly off the rock, and a single thread kept it tethered. Its twig case vibrated violently like a kite in a storm, dropped to the bottom, scrambled for a good grip, and got blown into the water column again. If fish were out and active that insect would have been eaten long ago. I wanted to explore more, to see who was out and who wasn't. To witness the life of the last part of the season. To see what was struggling to hang on and what was just waiting till water temperatures increased and the flourish of spring life ensued.

Sometimes the draw of snorkeling is the structure of the stream, the way water sculpts rock. Sometimes the draw of snorkeling is the force of the water itself, sometimes it's the life. This time of year it's more the first two. We seem to enter a biologic doldrums toward the end of January that lasts through the middle of February, where life becomes a little scarce. We were approaching the end of that dormant period, but were technically still in it on this trip.

Ice still formed on grass and twigs that hung low enough for the water to lap them, which resulted in oddly shaped ice formations hanging in midair. The creek water still hovered right around freezing. The air wasn't much warmer, so creek water readily froze to anything hanging into it and the dropping water level of the stream was evidenced by gravity defying bell shaped ice globs.

A mayfly clung to a rock next to a chunk of ice. I thought it had gotten the timing of its emergence wrong, crawled out of its old exoskeleton a new being a few weeks early, and died there stuck to the freezing rock. It was awfully cold out for an insect. But as I watched I saw one antenna move, then the other, and the mayfly inched one leg forward. It was far from dead; in fact its adult life was just starting, right at the end of the biological doldrums. Maybe it was the beginning of spring.

Waterfall Pool

The mountains of South Carolina are spotted with dramatic waterfalls and this one at Table Rock State Park was just as intense. The falling water made it loud, but beautiful. A new realm. A large school of some kind of minnow swam right up to my mask and camera, curious, which made getting a good shot difficult, but made the swim really enjoyable. The topography of the large pool graded from fine sand on the shallow downstream edge to a deeper pocket with exposed bedrock where the water continued to wear it away. A large pile of leaves accumulated on the right, under a canopy of overhanging rhododendron. A rhododendron branch swirled in the current, and I had to work to keep from being pulled upstream into the waterfall.

The stream funneled through a bedrock trough and dumped about 15 feet into the pool where a cascade of bubbles almost reached to the bottom four feet below. I picked my head up from the stream and a whole new view of the river revealed itself. I was almost directly under the small falls, and what appeared to be a modest-sized falls now seemed enormous. It was so quiet above in the forest, but when I put my face back under, the river was filled with the crash of the waterfall, like an unexpected constant rumble of a train.

It was loud and chaotic and the current twisted and turned and tugged at me. Every move had to be planned and deliberate, much like rock climbing. I made sure I had secure finger and toe holds in the smooth bedrock before I moved my right hand closer to the main flow of water. The current caught my legs and pulled them toward my head. This pool emptied into another ten foot drop and I was careful not to get swept over the lip. I was careful not to get swept down the ten foot falls. I held tight to the bottom as I got into the main flow and was amazed at the view, even though fine entrained air bubbles made things look murky. I thought I might have a new favorite subset of river snorkeling. I like downstream drifts and skulking where you start downstream and slowly work upstream, but snorkeling waterfalls is a whole other experience.

I was amazed because an incredible diversity of life swirled before me in strong eddies and lived in what seemed to be a pretty violent place from the surface. A group of minnows actively fed, unconcerned that I was there. A large stoneroller grazed on the bedrock shelf at the back of the plunge pool and darted behind the curtain of bubbles for protection. A school of 20 or so young bullhead catfish swirled in a large circle close to the bottom. Suckers faced upstream and looked like weather vanes pointing into the wind as their bodies changed orientation based on deflections of the current. Darters hunkered in the cracks in the smooth bedrock and a decent-sized striped bass darted through the center of the swirling current repeatedly. Sunnies hung on the periphery. A large eel startled me when it swam over my left arm and under my right.

"This is awesome," I said out loud, through my snorkel. I watched the different fish interact with each other, but mostly they were focused on how they interacted with the current. Like me, they were working to not get swept over the falls. The current was strong, and while it was loud here, it wasn't nearly as violent as it appeared from the surface, and a sense of calm came over me as I watched and experienced life happen. But the question of how all this life became established in a pool perched in the middle of the falls dominated my thinking.

I'd never expected to see all this biology in the strong current. I'd never expected to experience calm in the middle of a waterfall. But then creek snorkeling is good at expanding expectations. River snorkeling is all about exploration and experiencing the world from a very different perspective. It's about expanding our view of the world. And snorkeling waterfalls does just that.

Flying Wild Rivers

I felt like a squid as I pushed off from the shore into Muddy Creek a stream located in south eastern Pennsylvania. I took one large powerful sweep with my arms and legs, and jetted downstream. My plan was to fly a few miles of the Muddy Creek. The Muddy is a river not far from my house, but one I spend way too little time in. I call it flying because that's the sensation that best describes downstream river snorkeling

I reached the head of a class two rapid and swam a few yards further upstream into the middle of a large deeper pool. Bedrock jutted from the bottom and forced the water up toward the surface. Part of the pool has an extensive sandy bottom. I pointed my head downstream and let the current do the rest. While the force of the water was strong, the river moved slowly through the second half of the large pool. It picked up pace as the head of the rapid approached, and it got loud. The churn of water filled the underwater river.

I saw the surface of the water bend around and over rocks and when the drop was big enough, the smooth surface broke. Bubbles filled the water and disoriented so that it was hard for me to tell if my head was still pointed downstream, and more dangerously, it made it hard to see rocks until I was on top of them. It made selecting a route impossible and the river became completely in charge of which route I took. I had little say in the matter and could only fend off approaching obstacles. It was like riding a fluid roller coaster, flowing over around and between rocks. I was ultimately tossed through the rapid like a leaf, but was able to avoid collisions.

I quickly recognized that I was not in control, that I was at the mercy of the river. I relaxed and stopped struggling against it but rather went with the flow and let it help guide me around boulders.

The rapid became less violent and I glided through the remaining rocks. If I leaned right I turned right; if I leaned left, I turned left. Soon I was effortlessly flying through the river unencumbered by motors, paddles, or the hull of a boat separating me from the water. I circled out into an eddy behind a large rock, tired but thrilled.

I flowed out into a big deep pool. Ropy bands of smoothed schist plunged into the water as a sheer wall. Water carved chutes were too smooth to hold against the current and the eddy pushed me upstream, and then out into the main turbulent flow. I could discern the outlines of smooth, scalloped bedrock sheets eight feet below as I swam hard across the current to an eddy on the opposite shore and got swirled upstream again over a large peaked sandbar.

The circular current pushed me out into the main flow where I was swept downstream across the river into the eddy, then pushed upstream and back out across the flow in what would be a perpetual figure eight if I didn't grab a smoothed nub of schist in shallower water. It was a pretty incredible rush, akin to weightless flight.

I picked my head up out of the water and viewed the river from water level. I realized I was floating through a deeply cut gorge forested in old hemlock. It was secluded, and I felt like I was in the Pacific Northwest or anywhere else more remote than an hour from both Philadelphia and Baltimore.

A lot of the creeks I snorkel feel wild and that does something for my soul. When I snorkel these streams, I usually snorkel alone. There isn't anyone else around who I need to explain myself to, which is typical of most other streams I visit. These wild-feeling rivers flow through deep sheltered ravines. One of these places is Tucquan Glenn. When I'm there, I look over my shoulder frequently, just to make sure a bear isn't watching. Every once in a while a bear is reported from that region, and it makes the news since they aren't at all common. But still the place feels wild and remote enough that if a bear were to be in the area, it would like to be there.

While most of the streams I snorkel give off the feel of wildness, some of them truly are located in the wilderness. I seek out the large green expanses on maps—the wild places—because the rivers there are usually the most pristine.

One of the largest green expanses in my region is the Pocono Mountains. It was mid-summer and I was exploring stream protected by Natural Land Trust, one of the largest land preservation organizations in the east. Protected land usually translates to clear water and aquatic diversity. I was at least a mile from the dirt fire road I used to get into one of the biggest remaining contiguous forests in the Poconos. I kept hiking through the remote rhododendron undergrowth to find the stream that was marked on the map. The region had received abnormally large amounts of rainfall over the previous two weeks and water flowed down the trail. All of the rivers were flooding.

I could hear the rush of water from the ridge above and as I hiked down realized I was at the confluence of two streams. It took me more than an hour to get to this bottom hemlock forest and I was a few miles from the trail head that was a few miles from a road. I was on my own. Even a relatively minor injury like a twisted ankle in this setting becomes a big deal.

No one knew exactly where I was. I'd told my family the general area I was going to explore, but since I didn't know exactly where I'd end up, they had a couple thousand acre forest as my location. I was on my own in an area known to have active bear and rattle snake populations, and now flood conditions.

I scoped out each stream carefully to determine where I would put in. Safety was the primary concern. They were both running hard out of their banks by a few feet and flooded the adjacent hemlock forest. But the water was still clear. That's the beauty of forested watersheds; the reason I seek out the green spots on the map to explore.

If I started on the larger stream, I'd be fighting more water velocity and had a greater chance of getting swept downstream, with fewer chances for self-rescue. If I started in the smaller one, I'd have to deal with less velocity and would have more opportunities to pull myself out if I lost my grip on the bottom. I chose the latter.

I nervously geared up. My mask eliminated peripheral vision, and my wetsuit hood dampened hearing. I crept into the water, testing the bottom as I went. I didn't want any of the larger cobbles I was going to rely on to keep me from getting thrown downstream to roll away. I finally eased into the cold water, floated out into the current, and trusted my grip on the rocks to hold.

It was hard to hang on in the forceful current. My mask vibrated in the velocity. But the water was beautifully clear with a hint of orange tannins. The stream bottom was all large rounded cobble. I lateraled across the stream and explored each eddy, slowly working my way upstream using each tiny lee behind larger rocks to my advantage. My arms started to feel rubbery due to the constant strain of holding on and it was hard to breathe due to the force of water against my chest. The rounded rocks made getting a grip on one large enough to not roll in the current difficult. I peered out of the water frequently to see if a bear was in the area. I wouldn't be able to hear one if it were close due to the roar of the river. The water dropped into deep pools and flowed out in powerful flumes, and I used the hydraulics to help me move in the heavy flow. I saw a few trout trying to hang on in the current like me, but no bears. I got out of the river after an hour or so, exhausted and out of breath, and started the long hike out feeling fully alive.

The wildness, the deep holes and forceful chutes, all reminded me that I am just another part of the larger whole. Flying rivers, especially wild ones, puts me at their mercy and lets me know that I ultimately am not in control. And that reminder is one of the attractors to wildness for me. It shows me my place in the universe, that I am just another part, another player in the great cosmic unfolding. That I, ultimately, am not in control. It brings everything into a fine focus, and that acute awareness of the world around me, and my place in it, is living.

7. We Have Come Too Far

We came too far not to get in, I told myself, as I peered into the dark water of the Edisto River in South Carolina. The Edisto is America's longest free flowing blackwater river, so my family and I had made sure to incorporate time on the Edisto into a Christmas vacation to South Carolina. Blackwater says it all from a snorkeler's perspective. The water was over-brewed tea dark. It was clear, but orange-black, and I couldn't see much past two feet.

I stood on the bank in the January chill, looked into the dark water, and second guessed my decision to go in. But I have a hard time passing up an opportunity to get into a new river, especially one that is labeled the longest blackwater river in America. It is also one of America's most endangered rivers, and part of the reason for this trip was to get into the Edisto before it was too late. I really didn't expect to see much due to the dark nature of the water, but sometimes the allure of river snorkeling is experiencing the river from a different perspective, whether I see fish or not. We'd come too far for me to pass up the opportunity to get into the Edisto, so I waded out between cypress knees and eased myself into the fast moving tannin-stained water.

The river was cold and dark and my breathing reflected my chilly fear. There were gators there, though the chances of me seeing one were slim due to the cold temperatures. Even if I were lucky enough, it was unlikely that a gator would bother me. Still there was this kernel of fear in the back of my mind that came from being in unfamiliar, dark, cold water and it fueled my active imagination. My breathing slowed as the first water that slid into the wetsuit warmed and I controlled my anxiety.

Everything glowed red and cypress knees rose from the bottom like mountains in a hobbit middle earth world. The journey was rewarded with a completely new view. Even if I saw nothing else, that scene was worth it.

The Edisto's label of longest free flowing blackwater river unfortunately doesn't guarantee this amazing river's protection. People are competing for its water. Its fish are contaminated with heavy metals and other pollutants so that the consumption of some species can cause health problems. It receives unhealthy runoff and wastewater discharge. But we have come too far to give up on the Edisto, just like we have come too far to give up on protecting any river. The issues facing the Edisto face just about every river. Fracking places countless rivers at risk and needs to stop. We each need to take responsibility for the non-point sources of our pollution and correct it. Plant rain gardens and planters. Urge local officials to retrofit outdated storm water management systems to better control and filter runoff, and let your elected officials know that the quality of our rivers and streams are important to you. Get involved with your local conservation group, or the group working to protect your favorite river. Drive less. Finally, get into your local rivers and streams and appreciate them for what they are.

Our rivers aren't nearly as pristine as they were two hundred years ago. They aren't nearly as polluted as they were 50 years ago. We have come a long way with the passage of laws in the 1970's as part of the Clean Water Act and other regulations under National Environmental Policy Act, but we have a way to go. We have come too far and made too much progress to give up on our rivers now.

Mrs. Beck, my elderly German neighbor when I was growing up who lived across the Pumpkin Patch Creek in New Jersey, used to show me photos of stringers full of native trout that came from what is now not much more than a trickle of a creek. At the time she and her husband caught those trout, the watershed of that stream was forested and theirs was the only house. By the time I came to know the Pumpkin Patch, it was degraded by decades of suburbia. I still loved that creek, though, and I dreamt of a time when the Pumpkin Patch would be restored to what it was when Ruth and Carl first moved to Colonia.

It's about shifting baselines. My baseline, my memory of what defines a healthy stream, is actually a degraded condition compared to what once was. The information Mrs. Beck's photos provided was the only way I knew that what I perceived as pristine was far from it. I want my photos to serve the same purpose. I want my photos to remind us not to settle for less than what could be, because that's all we remember.

But unlike Mrs. Becks photos that show a lost abundance, I really hope my photos show a return to improved stream health. I hope my grandkids look at my portfolio and say "Can you believe how few herring there were compared to now?" I hope the baseline shifts to the positive.

Our ecological memory has a lot to do with what we perceive as "normal" in today's environment. How we recognize if our systems are becoming impaired is based on how we define normal, which is largely based on memory. It's heartbreaking to think that my grandkids might not even miss springtime herring runs. They might not even know they ever existed in order to recognize that they are missing.

The concept of shifting baselines usually pertains to ecosystems becoming impaired, and us not realizing it generation to generation. I'm finding that my baseline wavers back and forth, but generally that streams are in better shape now than when I was a kid. That doesn't mean we stop working for their protection. It means what we're doing is working, and we need to do more. Climbers Run is a good example.

Climbers Run is a tiny stream that flows through southern Pennsylvania farmlands. Parts of Climbers descends through remote hemlock and rhododendron glens. As soon as I got into the pool I saw a school of black-nosed dace ply the current in a swirling black, silver, and gold cloud. A sucker took one look at me and rocketed out of sight upstream. I saw two fish that weren't all that familiar to me just upstream of the dace. A pair of brook trout held in a hole next to a small log. Their colors were striking, with deep red bellies that graded to green mottled sides. Their crimson fins were white tipped and seemed to glow.

Brook trout are reversing the baseline here. Brook trout were native to our eastern streams. Sedimentation, warming waters, and non-native trout that we stock drove the brookies from many creeks. The Climbers Run brook trout were a mix of native fish and trout fry raised by school students in their classrooms in a program run by Trout Unlimited and the Lancaster Conservancy. They were part of an effort to restore Climbers Run to what it once was, and what it should be once again. This effort also included significant regrading of the lower section that had become significantly silted in, and the placement of trout habitat-forming structures. The release of classroom raised trout fry restocked the newly restored lower sections.

I don't have any memory of brook trout in the creeks I explored as a kid. I remember raw sewage and rainbow oil slicks. Brook trout should have been there. I didn't know they were missing. Brook trout in streams is a new thing for me. The norm were banded killis and black nosed-dace, suckers, and crayfish. The streams I explored were all impaired. Significantly. But I didn't know that. To me they were still these amazing places that held unlimited mysteries, and my attention.

I watched the brook trout swim beside each other in Climbers Run. I am still mesmerized by streams and my new concept of what normal should include. My memory of what impaired means is moving to the good and my baseline continues to shift.

Our rivers are in trouble and it's easy to become overwhelmed by the problems that threaten them: non-point runoff, erosion, eutrophication, drying up due to over-utilization of water, multiple competing user groups, invasive species. Rivers are embedded in huge complex problems without any easy answers, and it's easy to become discouraged. They're also embedded in our history and our culture. They provide the hope we need to carry on. To do the next right thing; to make a difference for water quality. River snorkeling is a beautiful tribute to the hope rivers provide and a call to renew efforts to protect them.

About the Author

Keith Williams is the founding Director of Education and is the current Executive Director at NorthBay, an outdoor-education program based in northeastern Maryland. He has a BS in Environmental Biology and an MS in Ecological Teaching and Learning from Lesley University. Keith worked as an Environmental Biologist with the US Army for ten years before starting his education career, and has conducted environmental assessments throughout North America, Southwest Asia, and Central America.

Keith has extensively snorkeled rivers in the eastern US, has developed a river-snorkeling based science curriculum, and has established river-snorkeling programs for nonprofits and the US Forest Service. He has led thousands of people on river-snorkeling adventures. Keith actively volunteers with his local fire department as a Paramedic and Swift Water Rescue Technician, and sticks his face in creeks every chance he gets.

www.ingramcontent.com/pod-product-compliance
Lightning Source LLC
Chambersburg PA
CBHW042015150426
43196CB00003B/52